GIVE BACK THE PAIN

Emotional Healing through
Source Completion Therapy

Robert T. Bleck, Ph.D.

Mills & Sanderson, Publishers
Bedford, MA • 1993

DISCLAIMER

The case histories and quoted passages appearing in this work are composites adapted from the real life experiences of Dr. Bleck and the many personalities with whom he has been in contact over his lifetime. They are used here for the universality of the emotions expressed, and are not intended to identify any particular individual or situation. All names and other specifics have been fictionalized to further insure anonymity.

Published by Mills & Sanderson, Publishers
41 North Road, Suite 201 • Bedford, MA 01730
Copyright © 1993, Robert T. Bleck, Ph.D.

Library of Congress Cataloging-in-Publication Data
Bleck, Robert T.
    Give back the pain : emotional healing through source   completion
therapy / Robert T. Bleck
        p.   cm.
    ISBN 0-938179-34-9 ;
    1. Affective disorders--Treatment. 2. Psychotherapy. I. Title.
II. Title: Source completion therapy.
RC537.b53   1993
158. 1--DC20   92-35216
                                                             CIP

Printed and manufactured by Capital City Press.
Cover design by Lyrl Ahern.

To my son Jason:

     I wish for the purity in your heart and the innocence in your soul to remain with you throughout your life.

ACKNOWLEDGMENTS

I would like to thank my wife, Bonnie, for her consistent love, encouragement and editorial expertise; my parents, Hank and Ruth, for their lifelong support and belief in me; Roseann Falcone, for her loyal friendship and her devotion to the concepts of SCT; and all those individuals who have had the courage and commitment to face their source.

Contents

1

The Wounds of Childhood

With tears streaming down her face, April paced outside the closed door to her parents' bedroom. As happened so often after her mother and father fought, her mother had stormed off to the bedroom and slammed the door.

The fighting was always intense and bitter. Her mother screeched and slapped viciously at her father, who clenched his fists, threw his arms out to protect himself, and stormed out of the house. Frightened, April desperately tried to find comfort with her mother.

"Mommy, Mommy, what happened? Where's Daddy going?" she whined.

Shoving April aside with her flailing arms, her mother responded, "Leave me alone you damned kid. It's none of your business. I want to be left alone. I just want to die."

Next came the banging of the bedroom door. Scared and feeling totally alone, April stood in front of the closed door crying and twirling her curly hair around the tip of her finger. As her body rocked back and forth, a moan made its way up from the deep emptiness within her.

Young, helpless, and paralyzed with fear, she was unable to speak, but inside her head she screamed,

"Mommy, Mommy, please don't shut me out. Please, Mommy, just love me, just hold me." Seven-year-old April stayed huddled outside the bedroom door, alone and trapped with her pain.

Conflicting thoughts and feelings raged inside little April. Part of her didn't want to be a burden and add to her mother's stress. She was terrified that with any more pain her mother might really die. Another part of April desperately wanted to be close to her mother at these times. She wanted to reach out to her, comfort her, and just make things better. If April could do that, then maybe her mother would have room in her heart to love April. Perhaps then, her mother might touch her, hold her, laugh with her, and treat her like a special little girl.

April yearned for such a warm, intimate relationship with her mother, but felt powerless to make it happen. So, not daring to upset her mother anymore, and fearing additional rejection, April sat huddled on the floor, holding back her tears and waiting for her mother to come out. Inside of April lay a well of unreleased tears and an emotional isolation so deep and consuming that it knew no bounds.

Twenty years later, April walked past her husband, through the living room, and into her own bedroom. She flicked on the light and stared at the clock. Her mouth was dry and her stomach queasy as she prepared herself for *the call*. It was Wednesday. She knew the phone would ring in 5 minutes. Like clockwork, her mother called every Wednesday night at precisely nine. She hated Wednesdays.

But maybe tonight would be different. After all, it was her mother's birthday. April had picked out a beautiful scarf and mailed it to her mother a week ago. She knew her mother liked scarves and hoped the gift would please her. Still, swaying back and forth and feeling nauseous, most of her really doubted it. When the phone rang, April suddenly felt cold all over as she braced herself for the hurt she knew would come.

"How are you, April?"

"Okay, Mom. How are you and Daddy?"

"Well, right now your father's trying to fix the dishwasher. What a joke. I'd fix it myself if I had the time. He's useless around here. I should have left years ago ... "

"Mom, did you get the birthday gift I sent?"

"Yeah, but I hate blue. You should've asked me first. You and your father never consider what I want."

At this point, April felt a crushing heaviness within her chest. Trying not to feel the rejection, April's eyes glazed over as she held back her tears. Her body stiffened, and she used her energy to keep her feelings of disappointment from surfacing. For the rest of the conversation, April responded mechanically, barely hearing what her mother was saying.

As she hung up the phone, April began to relive the feelings of deep isolation she felt as a child. Part of her wanted to reach out to her husband, connect with him, and be comforted, but—as usual—she didn't. Instead, she walked quickly out of the bedroom, past the living room, and into the kitchen. Reaching into the refrigerator, she pulled down the apple pie, cut herself a huge slice, and stood there eating ...

~ ~ ~

Closing the door as he entered his house, Steve noticed his mother, clad in a housedress, sitting alone in the dark. Switching on the lights, he heard his annoyed mother say: "Wipe your feet, put your school things away, and do your homework before dinner." He was hungry and wanted a snack first. As Steve took a step toward his mother, she threw up her arms and shooed him away like a fly.

Dejected, Steve moved back and thought how different his house was from those on TV. There, kids got a warm hello, a nice hug, and milk and cookies. Steve smiled for an instant as TV voices replayed inside his head:

"Hi Mom, I'm home."

"Hi Beaver, I'm so glad to see you. How about a snack?"

He really wished his mother would offer him such comforts when he walked in from school. "TV, what a lot of crap," Steve thought. Or was it?

The evening's dinner conversation, as usual, centered around the misdeeds of Steve's younger brother. Steve tried to interject a bit of information about his own day, but was sternly reprimanded by his father, who shouted, "Don't interrupt me when I'm talking to your mother. I hate that. I'll tell you when I'm free to talk to you. Now finish your supper."

Feeling wounded, Steve looked down at his plate, ate quickly, and then ran upstairs to his room. He grabbed his rubber ball and hurried outside. Steve started walking down the block, bouncing the ball hard and rhythmically as he went. As he made his way down the street, he strained to see in the lighted windows of the other houses. *What were these families like? Did other mothers give their kids milk and cookies? Did other fathers play ball with their sons? Were these houses like the ones on TV?* He desperately wanted to know.

Still wondering in his adulthood, Steve sat on the couch in his Manhattan apartment unable to sleep. At 2:00 in the morning, sucking and chewing furiously on the cap of his pen, he was feeling panicky. His third wife had left him and he couldn't understand why. He glanced down at his wrist and began to rub a new sore. *Suppose it was Aids. Suppose it was cancer. Suppose he had to go into the hospital. With his wife gone, who would take care of him? Who would reassure him? Who would feed him and nurture him?*

He thought back to his third wife's parting words: "I'm just so tired of our relationship, Steve. I'm tired of that distant stare you have in your eyes when I talk to you. You seem so involved in your own world that I feel you don't even know that I'm around. I'm tired of your lack of interest in me and your lack of response to my needs. I'm tired of having to ask you to hold me when I'm sad, and of you rolling over in bed when I reach out to you. I'm fed up with having to take care of the house, bills, and cars all by myself. I'm sick of constantly picking up after you. I hate being blamed every time you lose something. I'm yearning for a relationship with a man, Steve, not a little boy! I'm tired of being your mother...." Steve began rubbing his sore even faster.

What could he do to make these women stay? What could he do to keep their love? What did other men do? How did they keep their women? What was it like in other apartments? Steve rose from the couch, walked over to his desk and reached for the pornographic magazine and binoculars he stored in one of the drawers. Making his way to the window, he raised the binoculars to his eyes and continued his desperate lifelong search for love.

~ ~ ~

Helen heard the car door slam, and her body immediately tensed up. That familiar feeling of fear that started in her chest and burned its way outward to the rest of her body was instantly present. *What would he do to her this time?* She could try to hide under the bed, but when he found her the punishment would be worse.

At the dinner table, Helen dared not look at her father. She thought maybe she could make herself invisible so he wouldn't notice her. If she could stay as still as a statue maybe he wouldn't find a reason to scold her or slap her. Just maybe, she prayed. Maybe tonight it would be different. But it wasn't, and almost every night was the same.

Getting up from the table, he staggered toward her. Helen could feel his demonic eyes and evil smile come to rest on her. They were so penetrating and scary that to Helen he was the devil himself. She tried not to move, nor have any thoughts as he bent down to grab her. Grabbing her by the hair, he yanked her out of the chair. Her legs hit the underside of the table with a hard thud as he lifted her up with ease and dragged her toward his bedroom.

As they swept past her mother, Helen's eyes silently begged for help. But, as her mother looked away, once again Helen knew she would not be rescued. She felt trapped, powerless, and angry, but she dared not speak for fear of being beaten on top of what she knew was to come. She could not escape this house—or its horror— for 8-year-old Helen was also dependent on this man who was about to violate her again.

Pinned to the bed, she closed her eyes and tried to let her body go limp. She knew by now that if she resisted, the punches he would throw would bruise her face for days. First, he would tie her hands together with rope so rough that it cut into her wrists. Sometimes, he would tie her feet. Tonight, for whatever reason, he chose to bind only her hands, and she actually felt relieved; the trapped feeling was worse when she was totally re-strained.

As her father moved his fat belly on top of her, Helen gagged from his alcoholic breath. However, as he reached his hand down to fondle her, something hap-pened to Helen. It was as if she became a totally different person. She actually felt herself standing at the edge of the bed watching this horror happen to some other little girl; it was definitely not her. The bad girl in front of her must have done something to deserve what she was getting ...

Thirty-seven-year-old Helen woke from an unsettled sleep, startled and soaked with sweat. As she sat up in bed, her jaw was clenched, and she felt a sensation of heat building in her face. She began to beat her pillow. With every pound of her fist, a great fury rose up from somewhere within her, entered her head, and exited through her hands. Violently beating, thrashing, and twisting the pillow, a low animal-like groan escaped from her gut. She ripped at the pillow, cursing at it, and tearing away at it until its contents lay scattered about the room. Physically and emotionally drained, Helen rolled off the bed and onto the floor. Helen curled into a fetal position and, nestling herself as close to the window as possible, she waited for morning to come.

At sunrise, Helen got up and slowly headed for the shower. The water pouring over her body made her feel smothered. Uncomfortable, she rushed through the shower, dried herself off, and began her morning routine.

Every morning was the same. Helen systematically picked up each item on her dresser and nighttable, dusted them, and placed them back in their precise position. She had performed this ritual for as long as she could remember. It seemed to give her some sense of control, some sense of security. It helped her feel safe enough to get dressed and leave her house. But, safe from what, she always wondered. Helen had no memory of her childhood.

~ ~ ~

What do April, Steve, and Helen have in common? All three have grown into adulthood burying unresolved feelings from their childhood. Although grown up chronologically, their childhood pains continue to torment them and, at times, erupt in unhealthy ways. The cases of April, Steve, and Helen are based on real experiences of real people (all names and specifics have been changed). Although they may seem extreme, they are representative of what can happen when childhood wounds are left to fester.

To live a healthy and enriched life, our past emotional wounds—like bodily infections—must be cleansed and allowed to heal. *Source Completion Therapy* is designed to do just that.

2

What Is Source Completion Therapy?

Breathe ... breathe ... breathe ...," her husband gently whispered to her.

"Push now. Push harder! I can see the head!" shouted the doctor, still excited by the miracle of birth.

Nauseous and drained she wondered if she had any energy left. Ignoring the pain, and focusing on the reward of her labor, she strained for one last heave. With her body trembling and the blood rushing to her head, she pushed ...

"I have its head!" cried the doctor.

With one last push the baby slid out, still clothed in the warm fluids of its mother, and was assaulted by the new sensations of life. Cool air, the touch of hands, the light from the world were all new feelings.

Sucking the last drops of what had been life sustaining fluid from its mouth, the doctor cut the umbilical cord, separating mother and baby. Frightened, the baby took its first gasp of air. A new life had begun. Tears soaked the faces of both mother and father. They were tears of joy and awe at what they had created. Their eyes were alive with a brightness and hope—both for their child and themselves.

As babies we enter the world filled with sweetness, purity and innocence. Nature, in the form of our mother's womb, has kept us protected from the pain and hurts of life. And our eyes, as they open and begin to focus, are filled with a sparkling curiosity. Our skin, so soft and tender, even smells delicious. Though new and fresh, small and fragile, we are bursting with potential. Our little arms, hearts, and spirits are open to the magic and wonder of life.

As new human beings we are also helpless and dependent on our parents or caregivers for survival. We trust that our cries for food will be heeded, and our squeals of fear will bring comfort and reassurance. No longer in the womb, we trust that those charged with our care will keep us warm and safe from the evils in this new world.

If our cries go unanswered; if our needs to be tenderly comforted go unacknowledged; if we remain fearful rather than reassured, then that trust is betrayed. We view the world, not with wonder, but with mistrust and fright. The sweetness of birth begins to sour. Our spirits, once so open to life, begin to close. The potential, once so apparent at birth, begins to fade. Our journey through life may be one filled with emptiness and pain rather than joy.

In my work with people, I have seen how crucial the past is. Significant others and/or significant events in our lives can either ignite the flames of promise within us, or extinguish them. Furthermore, any pain, conflict, anxiety, fear or frustration that has been buried will linger and fester inside us. Like a growing cancer, these feelings will rear their heads in disturbing and dysfunctional ways. Obsessions, compulsions, intense rage, phobias, physical stress symptoms (headaches, digestive disorders, muscle tension, etc.) are clues to the deeper feelings that lie smoldering within us.

All of us possess a mental mechanism that consists of a conscious and subconscious component. The subconscious part wants desperately to rid itself of these cancers from the past that are trapped within our bodies. So repugnant are these feelings that they are often described as "ooze," "puss," "slime," "tar," "gunk," or "puke." Our subconscious literally wants to "vomit" this stuff out. However, the conscious part of us wants desperately not to feel any pain and tries to deny these feelings at all costs.

The battle that results between our subconscious and conscious can be compared to a pressure cooker. As emotional pain simmers inside us, anxiety, pressure and tension is created. Like a pressure cooker, a bit of emotional "steam" is released in the form of dysfunctional behavior (such as those discussed in the next chapter).

On the surface, behaviors like obsessions, phobias or addictions might not make any sense. However, they do have a purpose. They provide some relief to the subconscious while diverting the conscious from the original source of pain. If much of our time and energy is spent tormented over some phobia or addiction, there is little time or strength left to deal with our deeper hurt. Our conscious and subconscious have been temporarily satisfied. Tired, and with some pressure released, we have been able to avoid dealing with our deeper issues. However, as long as our original source of hurt or conflict remains unpurged, it will be necessary for us to periodically release our steam. Source Completion Therapy attempts to remove the "heat" source of our pressure cooker: buried, repressed feelings. Then and only then is the pressure cooker rendered inoperable. With the "heat" gone there will no longer be any "steam" to release, and our diversional symptoms will evaporate. Source Completion Therapy has been designed to accomplish that as you progress through its three phases.

Phase 1: Awareness

In Phase 1 of Source Completion Therapy (SCT), you will learn to explore, examine, and become aware of the main source of your dysfunctional behavior. As mentioned previously, most of us don't want to feel the pain of this source so we wall ourselves off from it with draining diversional behaviors. SCT, through a variety of techniques, shows you how to break through those walls and get to the true source of your torment.

When beginning this process with me, many of my clients claim to be aware of their "miserable childhoods." However, when I begin to ask them questions about the circumstances of their "miserable childhood," they are unable to recall large chunks of specific detail. Of course not; their conscious doesn't want to remember. Details such as places, times, ages, events, and specific people involved in their childhood traumas are often buried somewhere in their memories. Not being able to recall these memories, they often do not make connections between their past traumas and their present symptoms. They come to me seeking relief from these agonizing behavioral symptoms.

SCT attempts to lead the individual toward precise and distinct awareness. The more aware each of us is of ourselves and our background, the more we are prepared for the next phases of SCT. Many popular psychological theories or treatments stress that *awareness* is a *key* toward healing. In SCT, *awareness* is a crucial *first step*, but by no means the last.

Phase 2: Relive, Re-experience, Release

Phase 2 of SCT requires you to reach deep within yourself. No longer blocked off from memories of your past, you learn to relive and re-experience, in vivid detail, the events, feelings, and circumstances related to your pain. Through such varied techniques as visual imagery, meditation, and self-hypnosis, the intellectual process of Phase I becomes an emotional experience. You learn to focus on all five senses as you re-experience the sights, sounds, tastes, smells, bodily sensations, and all other related feelings of the past in the present moment. This phase of SCT brings the buried feelings to the surface, preparing you for phase 3.

Phase 3: Completion

As it's name implies, the third phase of SCT, completes the purging process. At this stage you learn to directly and effectively confront those responsible for your hurts. You learn how to give your "ooze," "gunk," or "stuff" back to their creators. I like to call this "giving it back to the source."

~ ~ ~

The entire method is designed to assist a person in becoming aware of their source of pain, releasing it from their spirit and body, and as a result, releasing themselves from the bondage of manifesting behavioral symptoms. Once the "stuff" inside is gone, mind, body, and spirit can be at peace. Purged, a person can then be open to the beauty and the magic that life has to offer.

In my work as a therapist, people have come to me seeking help with symptoms that are really only the surface clues to the deeper pain lurking within them. Those who have been hurt physically, sexually, verbally or emotionally tend to exhibit one or more of these symptoms, depending on the intensity, frequency, and duration of the abuse. These symptoms may vary in number and intensity at different times in a person's life.

The chart on the next page illustrates some of the more common manifestations of internal pain. A further discussion of these symptoms appears in Chapter 3.

Symptoms of Emotional Wounds

* Feeling inadequate, worthless, unloved, empty;
* Deriving self-worth and identity solely from productivity and achievements;
* Constantly seeking approval and affirmation from others;
* Being a perfectionist and/or striving to be perfect;
* Always feeling responsible for things that go wrong;
* Feeling intimidated by authority figures;
* Intensely mistrusting others;
* Feeling guilty, evil, or sinful;
* Fearing punishment for "wrong doings";
* Feeling and/or displaying intense and inappropriate anger;
* Withdrawing;
* Desiring to be in control at all times;
* Fearing intimacy;
* Being unable or afraid to express feelings;
* Having sexuality problems;
* Having obsessive thoughts;
* Having phobias;
* Criticizing and judging;
* Displaying compulsive behaviors;
* Feeling dirty;
* Having difficulty making decisions;
* Being detached, split, or blocked from feelings;
* Having intense dreams and nightmares;
* Thinking about suicide;
* Exhibiting multiple personalities;
* Feeling different from others;
* Having an addiction;
* Suffering physical ailments related to stress.

People afflicted with these symptoms endure such enormous suffering that I am appalled by the short-sightedness of many popular mental health remedies and therapies. They are far too inadequate to effect positive, long-lasting and permanent change for these individuals.

Cognitive theories advocate the "thinking" away of problems. They are champions of the power of positive thinking approach. Somehow, those who created these approaches believe you'll be able to wash away years of abuse and emotional pain. That's like putting a bandage on a festering, puss-filled, oozing wound. It might look nice, but it will certainly have a minimum effect on the healing process. The wound must first be cleansed.

Another image comes to my mind: sweeping dirt under your rug and putting garbage in your closet to make the room appear clean. Would you expect the dirt to disappear? Would you expect the garbage not to rot, decompose, and stink? Certainly not. The dirt and garbage must be dumped for the room to be truly clean. Similarly, the garbage inside us must be removed for true health to be achieved.

Behavioral therapies tend to work on the symptoms, one at a time. That's analogous to a tire tube overfilled with air and bursting with small bubbles. To depress one of these bubbles will only result in the bubble appearing in another section of the tire. The same principle applies to buried feelings. To work on just the outward symptom will leave these feelings bursting out and manifesting themselves in some other dysfunctional way. Remember, it was not the iceberg on the surface of the water that destroyed the Titanic, but the dangerous ice lurking hidden beneath the water's surface.

Stress management, relaxation techniques, hypnosis to relieve addictive behaviors, exercise and diet programs really only work on the surface symptoms, not on their causes. In many cases people simply substitute one of their old obsessions or addictions for an addiction to one of these self-improvement remedies. For example, a person might quit smoking after starting an exercise program, but become obsessed with exercising. This might appear to be healthy at first glance, but an obsession still indicates that there remain deeper feelings to be uncovered and resolved.

However, these self-enhancement techniques can be effective when used in conjunction with SCT. Once deep wounds are cleansed, you are open to enriching your life. It is now that a popular self-improvement method may be of great value.

Duration of the Healing Process

People first beginning the process of Source Completion Therapy frequently ask the question, "How long will this take?" The answer to that question depends basically upon four factors:

1. How buried, blocked, or repressed your true feelings are;
2. How committed you are to uncovering these feelings;
3. How courageous you are about facing and feeling the pain that you have been working so hard to avoid; and
4. How willing you are to give the pain back to its source.

The answers to these questions vary for each individual. Therefore, the time it takes to complete the healing process also varies for each individual. Very often the process of SCT is an uncomfortable one. You are asked to re-experience wounds, fears, and demons that you have tried to push away. You may start out committed and brave, but become resistant and scared along the way. This obviously extends the length of the healing process. It is, however, a normal part of this process and is to be expected.

~ ~ ~

Take a few moments to digest what you have read so far. Do any of the symptoms of emotional wounds apply to you? If so, how? What might be their relationship to past emotional pain? How willing are you to become aware, to relive, and to complete with your source?

3

Diversions:
How We Stay Unaware

As discussed in Chapter 2, our conscious minds don't like to feel pain. As a result, we have devised a myriad of ways to avoid, divert, and stay unaware of our emotional hurts and discomforts. Let's begin to explore the various diversions that human beings so often exhibit. Keep in mind that any diversion basically has two purposes. First and foremost, it is a way of staying detached from deeper feelings. Second, it does serve to temporarily release some of that simmering internal "steam" that results from our festering feelings.

Pronouns of Denial

Avoiding the use of the first person in our language is a very common diversion. A great majority of us speak in second or third person pronouns when we are really referring to ourselves. This kind of communication enables us to divert in two ways; we don't have to be consciously aware of our own feelings, and we can diminish the intensity of our feelings. Let's take a look at some examples.

The Pronoun "You"

Almost every client who begins Source Completion Therapy with me diverts from their feelings by using the pronoun *you*. The sample statements below are typical of people who use this method of avoidance.

> ...when *you* come home after a stress-filled day at work and *you* walk into a dark apartment, *you* feel so alone, so isolated from the rest of the world. *You* feel so empty. *You* just want someone to talk to; someone to touch and someone who will touch *you*. *You* just want some comfort ...

> ... How can *you* possibly live a normal life? How can *you* ever deal with others without mistrusting them? Especially men. When *your* own father would scream, rage, and slap *you* for questioning his control. He would hit *your* face if *you'd* laugh too hard. If *you* cried he'd slap *you* harder and yell at *you* to stop crying. When there was something *you* didn't want to eat he'd push *your* face into it, until the food made *you* choke. *You* tried not to say anything. *You* tried not to feel. *You* were petrified of being punished. *You* felt trapped by this ogre of a man and imprisoned by feelings of hatred *you* dared not express...

Now, let's repeat these statements, substituting the first person pronouns *I*, *I'm*, and *my* for the second person pronoun *you*. Feel the difference that speaking in the first person can make.

> ... When *I* come home after a stress-filled day at work and *I* walk into a dark apartment, *I* feel so alone, so isolated from the rest of the world. *I* feel so empty. *I* just want someone to talk to; someone to touch and someone who will touch *me*. *I* just want some comfort ...

> ... How can *I* possibly live a normal life? How can *I* ever deal with others without mistrusting them, especially men. When *my* own father would scream, rage, and slap *me* for questioning his control. He would hit *my* face if *I'd* laugh too hard. If *I* cried he'd slap *me* harder and yell at *me* to stop crying. When there was something *I* didn't want to eat he'd push *my* face into it, until the food made *me* choke. *I* tried not to say anything. *I* tried not to feel. *I* was petrified of

being punished. *I* felt trapped by this ogre of a man and imprisoned by feelings of hatred *I* dared not express ...

The impact of this substitution is striking. First person statements are so much more direct, personal, and intense. They are a potent tool for helping people realize the full power and passion of their feelings. This is crucial in Source Completion Therapy where feelings must be brought to the surface, experienced fully, and then ultimately released.

The Pronoun "It"

Another popular way people attempt to diminish the full effects of their feelings is through the use of the pronoun *it*. When we use this pronoun to describe our own feelings, it often sounds like we are referring to some creature or foreign being that is inhabiting us— like the deadly parasitic creature that attached itself to the internal organs of a human being in the movie *"Alien."* While attached, it received its life sustaining nourishment from the person. After a certain amount of time the creature metamorphosed, bursting out of its host. Shattering bones, muscles, and other organs in the human, the alien emerged—ready to begin its own life.

Let's take a look at a few examples of this simple diversion. Here are some feeling-oriented statements using the pronoun *it*. Underneath each statement I've replaced *it* with *I*. Once again, notice the difference in power and potency between the two statements.

It was embarrassing seeing my mother in that condition.
I was embarrassed seeing my mother in that condition.

It was scary when her car would pull up into the driveway.
I was scared when her car would pull up into the driveway.

It was frustrating trying to get my father to understand.
I was frustrated trying to get my father to understand.

It was painful when he left.
I was in pain when he left.

It was devastating when they divorced.
I was devastated when they divorced.

It was so rejecting when my own mother pushed me away.
I felt so rejected when my own mother pushed me away.

It was so lonely when he died.
I was so lonely when he died.

It felt so empty when she screamed at me.
I felt so empty when she screamed at me.

It was paralyzing when he touched me.
I was paralyzed when he touched me.

It felt like a prison.
I felt like a prisoner.

It was so infuriating when she tried to control me.
I was furious when she tried to control me.

In counseling sessions with my clients, pointing out this modest change in language always prompts an immediate and intense reaction in them. In many cases clients are shocked to tears. It is as if they are truly experiencing the feelings behind their words for the first time.

Third Person Pronouns

The use of words such as *we, they, everybody,* or *people* when talking about yourself, is another language diversion that waters down and diverts you from feeling the full intensity of your feelings. Read through the following few examples.

Everybody wants to be included and accepted.
I want to be included and accepted.

People don't want to be alone.
I don't want to be alone.

We're scared of being rejected.
I'm scared of being rejected.

Other Words of Denial

Words or phrases like *I think, I guess, maybe,* and *probably* have a similar effect. They allow you to escape the full power and ownership of your feelings. The next paragraph illustrates how masterfully diversionary language can be used.

It was painful when she rejected *you. You'd* try to touch her and she'd push away and rush off to the kitchen, where she could stay nice and busy and avoid *you. It* felt so lonely. *You* just felt so unwanted. *Everybody* wants to feel loved... *I guess* that's why it's so difficult for men to approach women. *You* just don't want to be rejected anymore. *You're* afraid they won't want *you* either. *I guess* a mother can really effect *you...*

Laughing on the Outside, Crying on the Inside

"I'm laughing on the outside. My smile is just skin deep. If you could see inside; I'm really crying. You might join me for a weep."

These profound and immortal words were uttered by the Joker, in the movie *"Batman."* The Joker was frustrated and rejected in his gruesome attempt to woo Batman's girlfriend. On exiting her apartment he recited these lines. Although I did find the movie both entertaining and humorous, I was also struck by the poignancy of these words; the use of laughter as a diversion to hide deeper pains is no joking matter.

I have been shocked by some self-help remedies that advocate *laughing* away your problems. The authors of these techniques believe you can heal yourself with humor. As with any diversion, this only serves to prevent your true feelings from surfacing. However, your escape from pain is only temporary. Your hurts will eventually surface in more intense, more disguised, and more dysfunctional ways.

~ ~ ~

During the beginning of one female client's therapy, she always laughed, smiled, and looked away from me when we started to talk about her father. Her father died when she was 8. As this client progressed through SCT, she began to remember the crushing experience of his death. No longer would she ride on his shoulders, and feel the windswept salt water spray her face as they frolicked on the beach. No longer would she feel the stubble of his beard when he tucked her in at night and kissed her on the cheek. When she cried out at night, he would no longer come to her room and stroke her hair until she went back to sleep. Who would comfort her now? Who would make her feel so safe? With her daddy gone who would tell her how pretty she was? She loved being his "special little princess."

After her father died, she often missed him and began to cry. Her older brothers, however, when they saw her start to cry, admonished her and told her to "be strong for Mommy." Her mother, not wanting to feel the loss of her husband, never spoke of him again. Scolded by her brothers for expressing her feelings, and unacknowledged by her mother, she felt alone in her grief. With no one to understand or help her with her anguish, she learned to stuff her pain back down whenever it began to surface. Laughter was one way for her to do this.

~ ~ ~

As a 50-year-old, one man was intent on making those around him laugh. On dates with women he would pretend to trip, stumble, and fall over furniture that was in his path, like a slapstick comedian.

Many times, these antics left his dates howling with laughter, and he would laugh along with them. However, beneath his laughter, welled a pool of tears. During SCT he began to tap into the feelings behind those tears.

As a young child he desperately longed for the affections of his mother, who was cold and distant. "I wanted her to hug me; to touch me. I wanted her to call me 'cute' and pinch my cheek, just like my friends' mothers did."

In grade school he began making his classmates laugh. Through jokes and slapstick comedy he tried to touch others. Perhaps, he thought, *they* would consider him *cute,* and in some way, touch him in return. He yearned for love, affection, and acceptance. His slapstick behavior continued until he entered SCT. Comedy never erased the wounded, empty feelings from his past, it only served as a temporary diversion.

~ ~ ~

I have also used humor as a diversion. Twenty years ago laughter filled the rooms of my fraternity house at college. A day or night rarely passed without some practical joke being played on one or more of the brothers. Laughter, beer, and girls flowed freely.

One day, however, I began to feel uncomfortable. The laughter seemed too loud and the practical jokes too vicious. People actually dumped others from their beds in the middle of the night in an attempt to be funny. Something felt wrong. There had to be reasons we needed to manufacture laughter, even if it meant being cruel. We did have reasons; we wanted to divert from our feelings.

We were scared of being drafted and having to serve in Vietnam. Those graduating were frightened of having to face the realities of work and responsibility. Those with girlfriends were afraid of commitment. Those without girlfriends were afraid of loneliness. Some were scared of failing and being forced to stay longer in school. Others were scared of passing and having to leave the home they had grown to love.

Some laughed away valuable and intimate relation-ships. Others tried to hide from past pain and hurt. Our use of beer and laughter developed into alcoholism and drug addiction for some of my brothers. As a student of psychology, I had some realization that we were avoid-ing our feelings. Still, they remained unexplored and unexpressed.

Some time ago, I caught the act of a TV comedian who left me feeling sad. Overweight, his entire act consisted of *fat jokes*. He described how he needed two seats when he went to a movie theatre, and how the pilots of planes asked him to move from one side of the plane to the other to adjust the balance. The audience was hysterical, but a deep feeling of sadness enveloped me; I knew he concealed pain beneath his jokes.

Sure enough, that very same week, this comedian was interviewed on a talk show. He spoke of how his father abandoned his family for alcohol and other women. He spoke of how he spent most of his life trying to use humor and laughter to avoid dealing with the desertion of his father. He tried to avoid feeling the crushing impact this had on him and the rest of his family.

~ ~ ~

During her sessions, one of my clients would consis-tently smile, giggle, and laugh each time she referred to any warm feelings she felt towards me. Closer explora-tion of her laughter revealed some of her true underlying pain:

> "... I don't want to feel close to you. I'm afraid of feeling intimate with you in any way. Laughing helps me block any of those feelings. If I connect and feel close to you , I'll be forced to look at the lack of love, warmth and intimacy in my own marriage. If I can stay numb from any tender feelings then I don't have to feel the pain of what I'm missing. In fact, I won't have to feel the pain of what

I always missed as a child; a loving, warm affectionate home. I'd rather laugh than cry; my tears would be endless ..."

Paraphrasing the late General Douglas McArthur; *Repressed feelings never die, nor do they fade away with laughter. They linger and turn to poison within a person's soul.* Laughter and humor can be an enchanting part of our lives. However they should be used to enhance and enrich life—to awaken our senses and feelings, not to dull them.

Most often, the simple diversions of laughter and denial pronouns are not adequate to suppress painful feelings. Our subconscious still fights to push them out, and our conscious still resists feeling them. Therefore, we resort to more intense, and more dysfunctional, diversions. The more energy we spend on a tormenting distraction or diversion, the less energy we have to spend on feeling our pain. Let's explore some of these more intense diversions.

Consistent Criticism and Judgement of Others

Feelings of dread used to overtake me whenever I chanced to see a certain ex-neighbor approach my house. Anytime he caught me working in the yard, he rushed over for a "visit," and the pattern of his oncoming assaults became well known to me.

First, he'd note that I'd had repair work done to my home; I could expect 20 minutes of torture as he criticized every facet of the work. When I had a deck built around my house he verbally attacked the entire structure: he negatively commented on the type of wood used, the kind of nails and braces used, the strength of the structure, and even the basic design of it. When any painting was done to the outside of the house, he criticized the type of paint used, as well as the color. If he actually watched the workmen, he commented on their laziness and inadequacy. If I did the work myself, he was certain to fill me in on what a bad job I'd done. The delivery of new furniture sparked special interest, as it availed him of the opportunity to rant about its poor construction.

Although I jest somewhat about my old friend, we all need to be aware of the purpose of his constant criticism and the pain that must have boiled within him. On several occasions, he spoke with me of his father's perfectionism. Whatever he did, as a child, his father criticized. His grades, though decent, were never good enough. Later in life, when he joined his father in the family business, he hoped to win his dad's approval at last, but he never did. Whatever he did, according to his father, was still not good enough. Whenever he spoke of his father, I saw the same deep sadness in his eyes that has betrayed countless others. He yearned for unconditional love, acceptance, and approval that never came. Criticizing others and focusing on their weaknesses and inadequacies keep many of us removed from our own hurts.

Remember: whenever we spend consistent energy judging, criticizing, and condemning others, there is little time left to look at ourselves.

During the early therapy sessions, many of my clients (of all ages) describe the diversionary patterns they saw in their parents while they were growing up. This example is typical.

Sitting down at the dinner table, the client—let's call him "Tom"—would be the first focus of his parents' attacks. They would start with the top of his head and work down. A fuss was usually made about his hair; it was either too long, too messy, or not combed to their liking. They would proceed to work down his body. His shirt was usually too sloppy, and his hands were not clean enough for dining. His parents would then move to criticizing his choice of friends, none of whom they liked: they were either too wild, too old, too young, or too irresponsible. Somehow, they were all bad influences.

The table conversation soon shifted to how ineffective the neighbors were as parents. When his parents were really on a roll, the assaults would center on entire races of people; Blacks, Jews, and every other ethnic group imaginable became targets. Nothing and nobody escaped as they worked their way through the overweight, the unintelligent, the poor, etc. Their hearts seemed cold and angry as they busied themselves maligning others. There was never time for warmth, intimacy, and honest feelings—nor room for love and caring.

~ ~ ~

Obviously, such attacks on others are a diversion from the deeper pain such people harbor within themselves, but my clients rarely understand that until later in life. Sometimes, during therapy, clients make an effort to talk with their parents about the pain of growing up in such an atmosphere. These discussions frequently reveal physical and/or sexual abuse one or both of the parents experienced as children. Once these secrets are exposed, clients more readily understand that flinging insults at others was their parent's attempt to divert from their own excruciating internal pain.

One of my clients began Source Completion Therapy by criticizing me, my clothes, and my office. He even attacked my sneakers. Commenting on their looks, he would call them "ugly." Next, he would proceed to attack their construction. The soles, insteps, and leather received about 5 minutes of abuse. According to him, my sneakers were not fit for any human being to wear. In fact, he insisted, *he* wouldn't put them on his dog.

Then, he would move on to my clothes. My choice of fabrics, colors, and combinations have been judged hideous—sometimes prompting questions as to how I walked out of the house without being embarrassed. In my office, all furniture, pictures, drapes, and office accessories within eye-shot has had to stand up under his scrutiny and criticism. He even hated the toilet seat in my bathroom; he thought it was too soft.

In cases like this one, therapy generally reveals that I am rarely the only target of such criticisms. Rather, almost all people with whom these clients have contact receive the same treatment. This man went so far as to condemn his wife for the type of clothes and toys she bought for their children.

As a child he'd longed to be close to his parents. He craved their affection and their intimacy. However, when he physically reached out to his mother for hugs, she pushed him away and told him she was too busy. His father was hardly ever home. When he was, the door to his parents' bedroom remained closed, although he sometimes heard them laughing. He felt shunned and excluded. He wished they would make room for him and share some of the affection they reserved only for themselves. He felt like an outsider in his own home. He wanted to be tucked into bed and kissed good night by his parents, but he was left with only his pillow to offer comfort.

As an adult, whenever his wife bought something for his children he felt jealous. He longed for the presents he never received as a child. He was competing with his children for his wife's attention and affection. Inside, he was still that little child whose needs were never met.

The more he criticized others, the less he felt this emptiness.

~ ~ ~

While going about my routine chores and errands I often overhear conversations between strangers. Sometimes the entire portion of their conversation that I hear consists of criticism. When these people run out of other people to criticize, they begin to assail institutions; the government, the post office, newspapers, television, teachers, hospitals, the police department, etc. all become the focus of their laments.

Comedian Jackie Mason, during his Broadway show, used to describe a man who intensely criticized the way his food was prepared in a restaurant: [Paraphrased] "I don't like the way these eggs are cooked. I told you soft, but not too soft. These are too soft. But don't make them too hard; they should still be loose. But not too loose; they should shimmer like jello, but not like soup. And these potatoes. There are too many crisp ones. I like a few crisp ones, but not too many. Put the crisp ones on the outside. The toast is too burnt. I told you dark, not burnt. I also hate my food touching each other. Keep everything separate. I told you some ice on the side, not in my soda, but there's too much here. Please take some out. But don't take out too much ..."

If you consistently criticize anything; people, institutions, food, etc. you are attempting to escape, in some way, your own pain.

Intense Anger Toward Self and Others

One day, driving down a highway near my home, I eased my foot down on the brake pedal and the car gradually slowed. Shutting off the air conditioning and opening the windows, I began to prepare for another of the long traffic delays that frequently guzzle my gas and test my patience. As a gush of hot air steamed in, I glanced at my wife and son with a resigned helplessness and began to fantasize that my car could sprout jet engines, zoom high above the heat and congestion, and land comfortably at our destination. My daydreaming, however, came to an abrupt end when I chanced to glance in my rear-view mirror.

A battered pickup truck sped toward my car, flashing its lights as it closed in. My mouth went dry, and my stomach tightened. Stretching my right arm over to protect my son and wife, I braced us all for a collision.

Miraculously, with screeching brakes, the truck slowed. Curious and relieved, I looked again in my rear-view mirror. The man driving the truck was yelling and waving obscene gestures at me. As he continued to scream, his contorted face grew fiery red. I was both puzzled and frightened. I scrunched up my shoulders as if in an attempt to protect myself from his assault.

Being as my car blocked the left lane, I assumed he wanted me to either move faster or get over to the right; neither was possible. Traffic was barely moving, and the cars were bumper to bumper in all lanes. Feeling trapped and helpless, and fearing for the safety of my family, I had no desire to slay this angry beast. And so, feeling somewhat protected by the body of my car, I tried to ignore this fury that raged behind me.

However, ignoring him only made him angrier, and he began to pound on his horn. As traffic began to inch forward, he switched lanes and pulled along side of me. "Learn how to _____ drive or pull over to the side so I can slap your _____ face," he shouted violently, looking through my wife and son as if they were not there.

Although frightened by this man's anger, I knew it was not really me he was mad at. He didn't know me. I was merely a convenient diversion for his anger. I was an excuse for him to release some of the *steam* that was eating away at his soul.

Perhaps you've been a part of a similar incident on life's roads and highways. You may have been a victim of the seething anger of others, or you may have actually been the angry beast—I know I have. In either case, intense, consistent, and inappropriate anger toward others is clearly a diversion.

Although unhealthy and dysfunctional, the use of anger as a diversion is both popular and effective. As long as you stay angry at some other person or external circumstance, you can stay distracted from any internal discomfort. The more time you spend angry at someone else, the less time you have for feeling your pain.

Obviously, there are times when anger is justified and appropriate. Understanding the difference between diversionary anger and appropriate anger requires an acute awareness. We will explore ways of making this distinction in Chapter 5. But, for now, let's take a closer look at how anger is used as a diversion.

~ ~ ~

As we rose from our chairs at the conclusion of our first session, I reached out to shake my client's hand in a good-bye gesture. "Don't you dare ever touch me," she hissed. Her red face and venomous eyes suggested that this poisonous anger had its origins in her past.

During the early phases of her therapeutic process, this woman looked desperately for reasons to be angry at me. At times, when I asked her questions, she insisted that I was badgering and pressuring her. She spent great amounts of time ranting about my insensitivity. Other times, when I remained silent, she fumed "This is a waste of time. I don't believe you care. Why don't you do something to earn the money I'm paying you?" When

I smiled, she would accuse me of laughing at her. When my expression remained neutral, she attacked me for being distant. Starting her session a few minutes late sparked her resentment. Opening the door of my office and greeting her a bit before her scheduled time made her feel "violated," and she mused about my intrusion into her free, private time. This client obviously spent a great deal of her time and energy searching for ways to be angry.

As she progressed in therapy, the reason for her anger became clear. Buried feelings related to her alcoholic and neglectful father were uncovered. Although part of her craved to be emotionally healthy, another part was desperate to keep from feeling this pain from the past. The closer her feelings came to surfacing, the more intense her anger became. By staying angry at me, she kept her focus diverted from her father.

~ ~ ~

During the 1950s it was common practice for many homes to have their milk delivered. The milkman, dressed in a sparkling white uniform, would place glass bottles of milk in a small metal box that stood outside the front door of each home. Watching the milkman move from house to house, visiting each of the many post-WWII families, was like seeing a Norman Rockwell painting come to life.

This particular Saturday, little 4-year-old David was excited. Today both his mother and father were home; he liked that. He always hoped that his father's presence would keep his mother from yelling at him so much. Whenever David thought of his father, he felt warm inside. He loved his father very deeply, especially when he got into trouble. His father never screamed or hit. Instead, his father talked very softly and gently, and explained just what David had done wrong. That helped him relax. He adored his father, and felt safe with him; he was scared of his mother.

Attributing magical powers to his father, he always hoped that—together—they could make his mother less angry. Then, on Saturdays, he could feel safe and warm with both of them. He could crawl into their bed, and they could all snuggle and laugh together.

When David heard the lid of the milk box close, he got a great idea. Feeling protected by the presence of his father, David wanted to try to please his mother, and make her happy. If he could do that, than maybe she would stop her constant screaming and hitting. David decided to bring in the bottles of milk, and take them to his mother.

Eager to please his mother, David took the two milk bottles from the box and headed for his parents' bedroom. In his excitement, he burst through the bedroom door and stumbled over his father's shoes, which had been abandoned on the floor. As if in slow motion, the bottles flew out of David's hands. His little heart pounded. David held his breath and watched helplessly as the bottles hit the rug, shattering into a thousand pieces. Glass was everywhere. Frozen with fear, David braced himself for his mother's reaction.

Startled and furious, his mother jumped from her bed. Her face turned ugly and monster-like. He knew her moving mouth was spewing fury at him, but he was too petrified to hear her words. When she reached for her shoe, David ran for the door. His mother hurled the shoe at him, but it thumped against the wall and fell harmlessly to the floor. David escaped, for the moment. There would be no hugs, laughter, or snuggling that Saturday. In fact, David knew he would have that same bad dream tonight. In his dream, witches resembling his mother tried to catch him and cook him in their big pots of boiling water. David knew he would wake up screaming and crying again tonight; it was always the same.

Thirty-four years later, David's mother tried to understand what went wrong. Racked with guilt and anger, she longed for an intimate relationship with her son, yet recognized that she had pushed him away. She loved him so dearly as a child. Why, then, had she caused him so much anguish?

During her therapeutic process David's mother revealed that she was raised by a tyrannical mother. She endured her own mother's tirades and beatings—assaulted by shoes, large wooden mixing spoons, belt buckles, and any other available object. Because she enjoyed athletic competition with boys, she was often called a whore and, on many occasions, she would find her sports equipment destroyed or thrown out with the garbage.

As she matured into womanhood, her mother often locked her out of her own apartment. Protesting her daughter's choice of boyfriends, her mother vowed to keep her out until the boyfriend was dismissed from her life. She spent many cold nights, huddling on the stoop, sobbing, and begging to be let in.

David's mother was angry. She was also pained by the cruelty, coldness, and lack of affection that existed in her home. Fearing reprisal, she dared not express any of these feelings to her mother—freedom of expression was not tolerated. As a result, she hid her anger and pain far from her conscious mind.

Although buried, these feelings were still alive within her. When she felt them stir, she would avoid them by using inappropriate anger toward others. Specifically, she used anger toward her son to divert from her true feelings about her own mother. Not dealing with the authentic source of her feelings had dire consequences. She regrets, to this day, the agony she caused her own son and grieves at the lack of an emotional bond between them.

~ ~ ~

Throughout history entire nations have diverted from their own domestic strife by directing their frustration and anger toward other nations. The syndicated columnist William Pfaff describes this concept well... "There is an old accusation that leaders like war because war distracts the public from domestic discontents. The fact is that the public likes war just as much as leaders do, for exactly that reason. War allows everyone to escape from their problems for a time. It poses a tangible challenge with a clear solution. War can be won. You can't say that about social and economic problems...."

Disgraced, humiliated, depressed, and starving after World War I, Germany diverted from its own internal struggles by focusing its anger on the nations of the world. Hitler's armies carried the banner of rage and hate, spreading evil and death wherever they went.

Eventually, political hatred was no longer an adequate diversion for Germany, and she turned her rage on huge segments of the population. This nation created an incomprehensible nightmare of brutality where demented political leaders, judges, military officers, and medical doctors served as role models. In concentration camps innocent people were tortured, beaten, starved, and gassed to death. Separated from their parents, children were used in genetic experiments, killed, and tossed into burning ovens. Blackened skies over the crematories stood in silent witness to Hitler's madness. Today, the entire world still mourns the millions of innocent lives lost to Hitler's "final solution," and agonizes over the horror of one country's rage and diversions.

Anger, when used as a diversion, is not always channeled at others. Sometimes people direct inappropriate anger at themselves.

Not wanting to feel the pain that was inflicted upon her by her sexually abusive father, one of my clients got angry at herself. Any imperfection in her job or her personal life evoked self-loathing. Being a few minutes late for a business appointment, or forgetting to put a snack in her child's lunchbox, would trigger self-directed rage. She would pull out huge chunks of her hair and pick at the skin on her legs until they were covered with crusty sores. When she was that angry at herself she could concentrate on nothing else. This diversionary tactic kept feelings toward her father buried and out of her conscious mind.

Remember: such intense, consistent, and inappropriate anger serves only as a temporary diversion, and may be destructive to yourself or others.

Obsessions and Compulsions

Like frenzied animals they clawed, tore, and grabbed at each other; so desperate for their bodies to join that they barely took time to shed their clothes. They could see, feel, taste, and hear only each other. Moans of pleasure were the only sounds they made, as their passion intensified.

With his wife out of town, Dan Gallagher, the lead character in the film *"Fatal Attraction,"* thought he could catch a few hot moments with Alex Forrest, a woman he met at a party. But, with the return of his wife, Dan wanted to be alone with his family again.

However, Alex was not ready to let him go. Out of touch with reality, she wanted to be part of his life. Only Dan's feel, taste, and touch could satisfy her. Desperate, she would stop at nothing until he belonged to her alone.

When he refused to answer her phone calls at his office, she began to call his house. He changed his phone number to an unlisted one, and moved his family to a house in the country. But, she refused to be *discarded.*

Like a predatory animal, she began to stalk him and his loved ones. Her obsession was joined by her rage. These two diversions were an explosive combination, which left in their path a wake of destruction. She doused his car with acid. She violated the sanctity of his home, and boiled his daughter's pet rabbit. The foreboding and uncontrolled evil was gripping.

If this had been real life, Alex's obsession and rage toward Dan certainly would have kept her distracted from any past internal pain. Although they helped her release some energy, they also kept her from dealing with the genuine source of her hurt. Separation from Dan could not have possibly caused her such intense anguish. She could not have loved him; she barely knew him. During their brief rendezvous, they barely had time to share anything more than their bodies. He was merely an escape valve for the torment she held inside.

Since the movie doesn't explore the social history of Alex Forrest, we can only guess at the original source of her grief. Was she *abandoned* by her father, or was it a former lover who hurt her? Perhaps it was her mother. Regardless of how and by whom she was hurt, her obsession with Dan Gallagher in the present kept her detached from her past. That's the purpose of any obsession; to keep past feelings suppressed.

Rising out of an individual's deepest recesses, an obsession can take any form: food, power, money, sports, sex, cleaning, work, etc. Anything that will occupy our minds and spirits can take the form of an obsession. And anything that shapes a person's behavior may become the focus of a compulsion. In fact, one obsession or compulsion might not consume enough energy to keep deep feelings buried. Therefore, an individual may resort to a variety of them, as illustrated by the following fictionalized cases of Carol, Ben, and John.

~ ~ ~

When feelings from her past began to creep into her awareness, Carol plagued herself with a tormenting ritual of obsessions, to divert from her surfacing pain. However, this left Carol with little time or energy for anything else. Any joy in her life was rare. Like some huge whirlpool, her obsessive process pulled down any present pleasures, drowning them with the pains of her past.

Carol began her ritual by obsessing on her physical health. A surface blemish, cracked fingernail, sniffle from an oncoming cold, indigestion, or any feeling of sickness would kindle this obsession. On one occasion, it took over while she was taking her morning shower.

As she washed behind her ears and under her neck, her right hand discovered a small bump just under her ear. The discovery sent shock waves throughout her body. Every cell, nerve, and muscle tensed in terror. She felt sure she was about to be punished by God; cancer was about to destroy her. She visualized her looks, energy, and spirit being drained away. She pictured herself dying alone in a hospital bed, withered and eaten away by her disease, the life support apparatus would be her only companion.

Summoning just enough courage to make a phone call, she arranged an appointment with an oncologist, for only a tumor specialist would satisfy her. In the days before her appointment, her life was a living hell.

Terrified, she became detached from reality. As if from another dimension, family, and friends appeared to her as vaporous apparitions: unreal and without substance. She heard their mumblings, but couldn't understand their words. Floating alone in some sort of *twilight zone*, all she could feel was fear.

Further weakened by her inability to eat or sleep, she cried constantly and attempted to bargain with God. If

He would allow her to live, she would pledge never ending devotion to Him and all of humanity. Her anguish continued until she met with the doctor.

According to the doctor, she had an enlarged lymph node which was no reason for concern. He even let her feel his, which had been part of him all his life. However, she would not be reassured.

Carol began to develop ritualistic, seemingly uncontrollable behaviors. These daily compulsions began in the kitchen. Walking back and forth over the floor exactly five times, she would grab the fifth napkin from the dispenser. First, she would fold the napkin in half, then in quarters, and finally in eighths. She would then open the napkin and tear it into five pieces. Placing these pieces on the kitchen counter, her fingers would flick them about for exactly 5 minutes.

Next, her hands would began a relentless exploration of the node, rubbing it with tremendous force. When they weren't glued to the side of her neck, they were turning the pages of medical reference books. She believed the lump was growing. Probing other lymph glands on her body, she was convinced the cancer was spreading and would soon ravage her entire body. She was certain the doctor was wrong, and she refused to trust his opinion. She became driven to find her own cure. Taking off from work, she would spend days buried in books, absorbing anything related to *her disease*. Finally, she demanded that her doctor perform a complete analysis of her blood.

The results of her blood tests were negative, confirming that she did not have cancer. However, as the doctor read her the report, she began to cough and feel phlegm rising from her chest. Panicking, she now felt certain that pneumonia would be her downfall. The hands of pneumonia, like the hands of death, would slowly choke the breath and life from her....

As a terrified child, Carol spent a great deal of time trying to find some solace alone in her bedroom. Wrapping herself in her bedding, she would stay huddled for hours. The blankets, however, could not shield her from the sounds. First, came the slaps. To Carol, it was as if those stinging sounds could pass through the walls, burrow beneath her blankets, and find her. The panic settled in her stomach and made her nauseous.

Next came the cries of her brother, pleading with his father for mercy. "Please, Daddy, please! Don't hit me anymore! I didn't mean it, Daddy! I'll never do it again!" The intensity of the sounds was always dependent on how much her father drank. The more he drank, the greater his abuse, the harder he hit, and the more thunderous her brother's cries. The anguish of these sounds filled her head, and her heart, with fear.

Terrified, she could hardly breathe. Muffling her own screams, she dared not move or cry out. She feared for her own life. *Would she be next? Would he beat her to death?* She always felt scared and vulnerable.

She did her best to avoid all contact with her father. She wanted to crawl inside herself and hide; she wanted to be invisible to him. Most of all, she wanted to silence the sounds that echoed in her head. She wanted to pack them away in a soundproof coffin and bury them where they could never haunt her again. So, as she grew, she interred both the sounds and her terror as deep within her as she possibly could. And there they stayed—festering.

Throughout the next 35 years of her life, these feelings often *leaked* into her consciousness. Not wanting to experience the pain, she used her obsessions and compulsions to hold it back. By consuming herself with worry, she allowed no room in her conscious awareness for anything else. Her obsessive fears successfully dammed back her past pains.

~ ~ ~

Ben began each morning exactly the same. The alarm clock rang at 5:00 a.m. Ben quickly silenced it by pushing the small brass button on top. He liked his old fashioned clock, because he could watch the hands move as he set them. He liked the control. He hated those modern clocks with their red digital time display. What he didn't understand and couldn't control always made him uneasy.

Jumping from his bed, Ben moved into the kitchen, filled the kettle with water, and placed it on the burner. Waiting for the water to boil, he wandered back to the bedroom and began his dressing ritual. He moved with the precision of robotic equipment on an assembly line. First, he wrapped his feet in socks, always covering the left one first. Next, he put on his underwear, shirt, and pants. After placing his wallet in the back right pocket of the pants, he took three quarters from his nighttable and, one at a time, let them fall slowly into his right front pocket.

Hearing the whistling of the kettle, he went to prepare his morning coffee: two teaspoons of instant coffee, boiling water, non-dairy creamer, and two tea-spoons of sugar. Every 30 seconds he sipped the coffee; he felt his body grow stronger and more energetic, as it braced itself to fight the day.

Energized, he reached for his Keds, which he always had ready by the front door. He took the vacuum cleaner from the hall closet and began to clean the living room rug. He made sure the machine ran over every thread of the carpet. When he was satisfied that the machine could remove no more dirt, he moved on to the other rooms of the house, giving them the same attention. He worked carefully until he was convinced that the machine could gobble up no more dirt. Then, using a hair comb, he crawled around on his hands and knees searching for any dirt the machine might have missed. Eventually, when he was certain the rugs were clean, he headed for the front door.

Once in the garage, he snatched the two rags from their separate hooks. Tenderly, he poured some Ivory liquid soap into a half filled bucket of warm water and began to clean his car.

He dipped one of the rags into the bucket and began to caress his 1962 Chevrolet. Gently and meticulously, he cleaned every crevice of the car. Soaking up the excess water with the dry rag, he then polished his car until it sparkled. Placing everything back in its proper place, he got into his car and set out to face the world.

When SCT forged an opening into Ben's awareness, numerous memories flooded in. Like thunderous waves, painful images from his childhood crashed onto the shores of his conscious mind. In SCT he realized that these images from the past had been kept submerged by his obsessions and compulsions. He orchestrated those diversions to drown the details of his hurtful childhood. However, like some immortal beast, his memories lay in wait within him.

One of his most painful memories to surface centered around his mother's absolute coldness. When he was sick, she would enter his room very quietly. Mechanically, without a smile or a spoken word, she would leave aspirin and orange juice on his nighttable. Her eyes stared right through him, as if he were a ghost. He never felt that she really looked at him; her eyes seemed to ponder something far away. They never appeared to see him as her 7-year-old son. To him, they were icy, cold, and impenetrable; and they scared him. He was never able to melt those eyes and feel her warmth. Instead, like a stranger in his own house, he felt discarded.

Driven solely by her sense of obligation, she rearranged the blankets covering his body, turned on the vaporizer, and walked out of the room. Inside, he cried out, "Mommy, please don't leave. Stay and love me." Although his body throbbed from the flu, he suffered more from the ache in his heart. The steam from the vaporizer was the only warmth that surrounded him at night. His pleas for affection went unanswered, and his loneliness remained unsatisfied.

For as long as she lived, his mother's eyes remained just as frozen, and her stare just as distant. He never could understand or control her any better than those digital clocks he hated so. So, for the next 43 years, Ben used his diversions to drown the rejection and pain. Each second of every day he shrouded himself in the fog of his obsessions and compulsions, leaving no time free to feel his hurt.

~ ~ ~

Waiting for the train, John walked over to the exact spot he had occupied for the past 5 years. As he took up his position, he spotted the abandoned wad of half-chewed gum that had kept him company for so long. Staring at the gum, he began to feel uneasy. Discarded by someone, this small piece of candy was so sad. Without the slightest regard for its existence, the heels of shoes trod upon it as they went about their daily business. It now lay embedded in the section of concrete over which he loomed. Alone and dirty, it offered no resistance to the sorry treatment it received. For an instant he identified with the gum. He was relieved to hear the train's whistle signal its arrival.

The great mechanical doors hissed open on car number 20, and John slipped effortlessly into his place. He had repeated the same motions for so long that he moved about without thinking; his body had memorized the routine. Counting the eleven steps to his seat, he shed his coat, removed the book from his briefcase, sat, and began to read. Absorbed in the book, he felt no longer carried by the train, but by the bending and twisting of the plot. The author's world was now his, and he was conscious of nothing else.

While still in his fantasy, the train reached his destination and John headed toward work. At his office, the lights from his desktop computer seemed to call to him, like a close friend cheerfully calling out a welcome. He was excited to see her and could almost feel her smile. She would entertain him for the morning hours. In fact, they would please each other. As he caressed her keyboard, those sweet little letters would dance and sing for him. Like a sensual coupling between two lovers, they satisfied each other's needs until lunchtime.

After five such pleasurable hours, he gently stroked the monitor and disengaged. Separated from his morning lover, he was now prepared for the afternoon.

Like part of a *Star Trek* movie, John seemed captured by some cosmic tractor beam. Unable to break free, he felt himself drawn into the sleazy section of the city. Although feeling out of control, his body also tingled with desire. His heart pounded in anticipation. His dry mouth and throbbing groin knew that soon they would be pleased. Prostitutes, drug pushers, adult pornographic palaces, and massage parlors would become his mid-afternoon diversions.

Dodging both the summoning calls of men selling drugs, and the alluring incantations of young women in short skirts and high boots, he weaved into one of the adult bookstores. As he browsed the aisles, his eyes feasted on a delectable assortment of women; all seductively exposed in a variety of positions. The saliva began to drip from the corner of his mouth, as he moved from one tempting picture to the next.. At the back of the store, he shoved aside the dirty curtain and entered one of the small cubicles. Here, directly in front of him was another curtain. As he put some change in the slot to the right, the curtain lifted and revealed a glass partition. Here was what he had come for; a very young woman, or perhaps a girl, clad in a skimpy, glittery costume, and dancing just for him. He stared, drooled, and longed to touch her. After 3 minutes the curtain came down, leaving him disappointed. He put some more change in the slot.

Sometimes, after the second dance, John would make his way to a woman he could really touch. Finding a massage parlor, he would pay a lot more money to be fondled and rubbed for an entire hour.

Soon lunchtime was over, and he returned to work. Back at his office, he almost felt like a cheating lover. Moving rapidly past the people, he switched on his computer to signal his return. He felt glad to be back with his friend. He would make it up to her. For the next 5 hours they would stay locked in a heated digital embrace.

Long after dark, as 10:00 p.m. approached, he reluctantly decided it was time to return home. Waiting on the platform for his train home, he made reassuring contact with his book, and held it in both hands. The doors to his railway car slid open and swallowed him up once again. He walked to his seat, and dreamily thought of the computer that waited patiently for him at home. Sitting, he opened his book, and began to read...

SCT helped John realize the purpose of each of his obsessions and compulsions. The product of a parental divorce, he felt deprived of his father's love, guidance, and encouragement. "With my father gone, I felt a deep, dark, empty well within my chest," John told me.

Rather than filling this hole with her affection, his mother actually made it deeper. Selfish and needy herself, she was emotionally and physically removed from her son. John often remembered the sadness he felt during his childhood baths. Soaking in the tepid, sudsy water, his little body ached to be surrounded by the warmth of his mother's arms. He longed to splash and play with her.

However, those were comforts John never experienced. Instead, she did her best to avoid all contact with him. Her arms remained locked at her sides, and any warmth he received came from the running water. Silently, she handed him a washcloth, and told him to wash himself.

When he finished bathing, his body was clean, but he felt dirty inside. Cut off from his mother's touch and intimacy, he felt like he had a contagious disease. He felt untouchable, and believed he would contaminate all those with whom he had contact. John ached with isolation, anger, and frustration.

Instead of the dirt, he wanted to wash the pain down the bathtub drain. But, as a young child, he just didn't know how to accomplish that. So, he poured all his hurts deep within that well in his chest, and hoped they would never surface again. As he grew, he would use his obsessions and compulsions to keep them submerged. Reading, work, and pornography served as separate, but equally powerful forces. They squelched any feeling that periodically worked its way up from the well and attempted to surge into his conscious.

Carol, Ben, and John all suffered from obsessive-compulsive behavior. Like the rising moon, and the ebb and flow of the tides, their obsessions were seemingly uncontrollable. Like beating hearts, their compulsions were consistent, rhythmic, and powerful. Tormenting by themselves, obsessions and compulsions serve to divert from deeper discomforts; the former by consuming thoughts and the latter by consuming behaviors.

Addictions

The protective darkness of the casino lured him in. Like a sorceress, it shielded him from the harsh daylight and provided an escape from the realities of life. All it asked of him in return was to roll the dice.

Bending over the crap table, his nostrils caught the pungent scent and he smiled. He loved the smell of cigar smoke. To him, it was the smell of success. He associated it with the gratifications of money, power, and beautiful women; all luxuries which he lustfully pursued.

He felt comfortable here. The chattering chips and the clinking bar glasses seemed to call to him. As his eyes followed the drifting cigar smoke to the ceiling, the glistening chandelier winked at him. Here, he felt like he belonged.

The stickman pushed him the dice. Tenderly, he picked up the red cubes, and rubbed them between his palms. He began to shake the dice vigorously. Stirring them stirred his passion as well. His body felt energized as he prepared to release the dice. Nothing else mattered, not even his former friends or family. Like the cigar smoke, they just seemed to drift away, break apart, and vanish from his life. But right now, he didn't care. With a tremendous thrust, he threw the dice ....

Gambling can become an addiction, and the purpose of any addiction is to divert ...

Years ago, I had a college friend who was a sensa-
tional baseball player. As a freshman, Paul was nick-
named "Hustler" by his coach; it was an honor denoting
good old-fashioned American grit and determination.
He was a fierce competitor, bursting with talent, and that
same year he led his baseball team in four areas; hits,
RBI's, extra base hits, and triples. His magnificent
hitting was equaled by his spectacular performance in
the outfield. Sprinting, diving, rolling, and crashing into
fences, Paul would risk life and limb to rob opposing
players of an extra base hit. The potential symbolized by
the Outstanding Player trophies he received in high
school was being realized in college.

The achievements of his freshman year were omens
of even more success. Named captain of the team, Paul
continued to dazzle coaches, players, and fans with his
remarkable skills and electrifying enthusiasm. The
small college stadium swelled with excitement as ador-
ing fans chanted in tribute to their local idol.

Seeing the professional scouts and recruiters come
to watch Paul play, I believed that the sport of baseball
would provide him with fame, fortune, and immortality
in the record books. I would often hum the tune to some
current commercial jingle, and visualize major compa-
nies using his name, face, and reputation to endorse their
products. I thought, for sure, that Paul was destined to
become a God of the diamond.

Although I didn't always make it to the ballpark to
see Paul play, when I did, I felt like I had a seat in heaven.
Captured by the sights, sounds, and magical spell of
baseball, I would often flash back to my own Little
League days, and for brief moments, I was truly back in
time ... Steadying myself at shortstop, I could smell the
fresh cut grass and feel the warm summer sun on my
cheeks. Intently watching the pitcher throw the ball, I
saw the batter swing and heard the crack of the bat.

Instinctively, my body responded. Scurrying to over-take the ball that was hit in my direction, my feet kicked up a cloud of dirt. Gracefully, I caught the ball. In a fluid motion, I planted my feet to the earth, grabbed the ball from the glove, and threw to first base. The smack echoed from the first baseman's glove before the runner's feet thumped against the base. The batter was out and I was triumphant.

What glorious memories. Immersed in nostalgia, peanuts, and Paul's baseball prowess, I was provided with an afternoon of contentment. I was very grateful to Paul.

It was during his junior year that our relationship, as well as his sparkling potential, began to dull. During one game, a small battle erupted between Paul and the opposing shortstop. The agile, but frail shortstop was no match for Paul. After colliding at second base, Paul charged into the smaller man. Overwhelmed, the short-stop tumbled to the turf. Like a steamroller, Paul rolled over the sprawled ballplayer. For a brief moment, my attention was drawn to Paul's eyes. I was frightened. The eyes were filled with anger, and I was glad for the protective distance between us. About to have his life squeezed from him, the downed man was rescued by his teammates and the umpires. The confrontation confused me. *What would provoke my friend to the point of using his power to such an unbalanced advantage?*

Teammates, coaches, and fans dismissed his out-burst by attributing it to the passion and pressure of the game. They credited his violence to his intense desire to win. They admired him. I, however, remember feeling that something deeper lay buried beneath Paul's eyes; something that had nothing to do with our national pastime. It had nothing to do with hits, runs, stolen bases, or RBI'S. What I felt was much more personal than a game.

Outside of the stadium, removed from the roar of the crowds and the radiance of the lights, Paul began to play quite a different game. He sometimes invited me to join him, and I did just once.

Paul's arena outside the bright ballpark was a shadowy and unsavory playground. Like the moist, musty space under decaying vegetation, this playground seemed to breed its own cluster of frightening creatures. At his favorite sleazy hangout, individuals bordering on the immoral, deceitful, and corrupt attracted Paul like strong magnets. The glistening of rings, necklaces, bracelets, and watches adorning these men was in sharp contrast to the dirty whiff of criminality that enveloped them. Wallowing in such an unscrupulous atmosphere, Paul nourished an addiction to gambling. As he spent his hours betting on all sporting events from baseball to bocci, Paul's career slid not into the record books but into decay.

More and more withdrawn from his teammates, classmates, and former friends, his addiction robbed him of strength and energy, and his performance on the field began to suffer. Paul's gambling led to trouble with school administrators and, eventually, the law. The number of professional scouts that came to see Paul play dwindled. The cheers that once shook the stadium grew silent.

For Paul, there would be no commercial products to endorse, no civic groups to motivate with inspiring speeches, no chance to be honored by the Baseball Hall of Fame, and no signing of baseball autographs for awestruck kids.

During those seasons of long ago, I was a rookie apprentice at my own craft and didn't quite understand why Paul would toss away a shot at such a shining future. Today, as a veteran in my field, I would be willing to bet that Paul's addiction to gambling was a diversion.

According to Paul, his father was a baseball fanatic who was trapped in a job he hated. Like himself, he wanted Paul to be interested in baseball, and at an early age, began grooming him for stardom.

Almost every waking moment was devoted to baseball. Paul was forced to spend much of his evenings and weekends hitting, bunting, running the bases, fielding grounders, and catching pop flies hit by his father. The pace was relentless. Often, Paul was pushed to exhaustion, or allowed to stop only when parts of his little body bled. No matter what the cost, it appeared that Paul's role in life was to rescue his own father from a life of drudgery and obscurity.

When they weren't playing ball, they watched it on TV. Whatever time remained was spent collecting baseball memorabilia and wallowing in the statistical accomplishments of both past and present performers. As Paul grew and played organized baseball, from Little League to High School, his father sat staring in the stands and continually charted his progress.

Did Paul feel pressured during his childhood days? Did he feel that his worth as a human being depended on how far he threw a baseball? Did he feel that the amount of recognition he got from his father depended on his batting average? Were the hugs of affection he got from his father akin to his on-base percentage? Did Paul grow up believing that his internal self-worth depended on how much he produced on the ballfield? Did he feel inadequate unless he was performing and pleasing his father? I think so. I think that feeling accepted only for what he produced rather than for who he was pained him deeply.

But Paul didn't want to feel his pain. He wanted to feel his father's love. So, he stuffed down his hurts and dedicated himself to the sport of baseball. For a long while, Paul's commitment actually served as an asset.

His obsession with baseball sparked a dedication to be the best at his craft. Perhaps, he thought, by accumulating all the thrills, frills, and accomplishments in the baseball world, he could somehow fill his sense of internal worthlessness. Perhaps he might be able to make up for the unconditional love his father never gave him.

However, although Paul's diversion with baseball made him Big Man on Campus, and helped him attain admiration and success for a time, it apparently was not enough to quell the discomforts that still bubbled inside him. In a further attempt to keep his pain from surfacing, he turned to gambling. It was this addiction that wreaked havoc on his chance at baseball immortality. Gambling drained him of all that wonderful potential and left him floundering in ruin.

~ ~ ~

I lay on the subway
    sick to my stomach
    and wonder what did I
    do to deserve this life.

I wanted my mother
    long dead in her grave
    to save me from strife

I robbed and used people to criticize
    and abuse and now
    I sit not deflecting and
    must muse.

If only my mother had
    given me her nipple,
    I would not have to
    turn and drink more ripple.

This poem, titled *"Urge for Ripple,"* was written by a 50-year-old alcoholic man. As he discovered in SCT, his present day agony had its roots in his infancy.

The crib was placed in a dim hallway. Isolated from the main rooms in the house and devoid of human contact, it sat in darkness.

For a few moments he was fascinated by the shadows. His eyes followed them as they pranced along the hallway walls. Bending and swaying, the shadows reminded him of the close presence of life. He felt teased by the images of these people he could not touch. He wanted more than just their flat, distorted, reflections, he wanted them.

He wanted them to take him out of his lonely world. He craved the warmth of their affection. Unfortunately, his cravings went unfulfilled.

Trapped by the bars of the crib, he screamed for attention, and shook the bars that held him captive. "I was angry. I wanted to be acknowledged. I wanted the shadows to come alive. I wanted my Mommy. My hands shook the bars with all the strength my small body could produce." The sound of the rattling crib mixed with his own cries for love, but his mother never entered the hallway. Only her elusive shadow kept him company. Drained from his hours of effort, he fell to the cushiony bottom of his cage. Whimpering and gasping for breath, he gave up his fight. Finally, when it was time for his feeding, the maid walked into the alcove, and prepared him for the meal ...

With the passage of time he outgrew the constraints of his infant prison. However, his parents grew no more emotionally close than their black figures on the wall. Overwhelmed by the chasm of emptiness his parents helped dig, he desperately sought comfort. He sought to erase those evasive spectral images and accompanying feelings of isolation from the walls of his mind. He wanted to create a place where he felt loved. He wanted to feel the comfort of human bonding. On his own, however, he had difficulty in creating such a world and in snuffing out the pain from his past. Those bleak images and feelings continued to whirl within his subconscious. As a result, whenever they made their way into his consciousness, he drank. Alcohol became a deceptive friend, teasing him with visions of the peace and love he longed for.

However, he remained a prisoner. Still trapped by the nightmares of his childhood, he became further incarcerated by his destructive dependence on alcohol. This vicious cycle entwined him in chains of torment that were impossible to break.

~ ~ ~

As with alcohol, diversions through drug abuse and smoking also trap the individual in a physiological dependence. Withdrawal from any of these addictions may result in minor physical discomforts or agonizing withdrawal symptoms. Excessive sweating, intensified desire for the drug, vomiting, diarrhea, muscular cramps, severe headaches, tremors, insomnia, dehydration, delirium, and hallucinations are among the physical demons addicts may face in their efforts to break free of their addictions.

Many institutions, schools, courses, media programs, hospitals, corporations, private individuals, and government agencies have devoted money and energy to research, treatment and cure for those so physiologically dependent. As a result of their efforts, volumes of information have been written, disseminated, debated, and discussed. Some of their beliefs and philosophies have been put into practice. I strongly contend that any treatment program must consider the source of pain beneath the addiction. Not to do so will result in a person craving comfort from their original addiction, or eagerly thirsting for another diversion. The source must be effectively faced and confronted for recovery to be permanent.

~ ~ ~

She hated the stars. Their twinkling brightness brought with them the contrasting darkness of the night. It was this darkness that routinely awakened the fear that resided within her.

Each evening, with the setting of the sun, the terror began to stir. Aroused by the darkness, she could feel her fright taking shape. At first, she would feel nauseous. Then, the terror rose up and made its way through her body. As it worked its way toward the light, her terror grew stronger. She wanted to scream, but her throat closed up in fear.

Huddling her little 7-year-old body close to the wall, she kept the blanket pulled over her head. Forbidden to close her bedroom door, she took one last look at the light that filtered in from the hallway. Shutting her eyes, she lay shivering ... and waiting.

She sensed his presence immediately. His huge body blocked the light from the hall and cast a shadow on her face. Her cheeks had the sensation of being pricked with little pins. The floorboards creaked as he moved closer, and she heard his heavy breathing. She used what energy she had in her control to breathe rhythmically and pretend to be asleep, for if she moved he usually stayed longer. Once beside her bed, he lifted her blanket and nightgown. Sliding his monstrous hand along her young smooth leg, his fingers moved between her legs, then up to her chest, where he began to pinch and fondle her breasts. Her screams of protest and violation lodged in her throat. She prayed it would be over soon.

After about 3 minutes, he left. These few minutes of violation were the only time she ever felt her father's touch. In the daylight he was an intimidating stranger. With the same passion that she hated the stars, she hated her father as well.

As she grew a bit older, her father stopped feeling her at night. With her advancing age, he decided to direct his hands to her younger sisters. Although this overpowering giant stayed clear of her bedroom, feelings from his toxic touch remained in her body.

Feeling contaminated, she wanted to purify herself. Searching for an antidote, she discovered one that was readily available, relatively safe, and—best of all—numbing. With each mouthful of food, she washed down her feelings; each sliver weighted down her feelings and dragged them to the farthest regions of her being. And this is where she worked to keep them.

Her antidote became her addiction. When her feelings worked their way into her conscious awareness, she started to eat. She used food to keep herself numb, diverted, and unaware of the true source of her pain.

However, her subconscious wanted to throw off these awful feelings—to purge them from her body. But, her conscious was still in command, and wanted any purifying process to be quick and emotionally painless. On some occasions, after an enormous binge, she would move dazily into the bathroom. Sticking her fingers down her throat, she tried unsuccessfully to compromise with her subconscious by vomiting up her feelings with her food. But, only the food streamed out with her vomit. Her toxic feelings remained. As a result, she continually needed food to smother them.

Phobias

The water blasted her windshield like tiny shotgun pellets. Each raindrop exploded with deadly fury as it smashed against the glass. The wipers were just temporary safeguards, streaking away the droplets, only to have more take their place.

To her, the threat was real. The muscles in her body constricted with tension. Her jaw locked, and her hands squeezed the steering wheel. Terrified, she imagined each wave on her windshield wipers striking out at her. She visualized every minuscule drip, bursting with millions of virulent germs, each eager to explode onto her skin. So attached, each lethal germ would bore its own tunnel into her bloodstream. Here they would begin their feast. Drinking her blood for strength, they would render her healthy corpuscles and antibodies useless. With their newly found power, they would stream to the various organs in her body, and proceed to devour them. Their rapidly moving incisors would pierce, rip, and chew through her. Showing no mercy, they would take her life and lick their voracious lips in the process. It would all be over in a matter of minutes.

As she came out of her terrified trance, she tried to concentrate on the road. The squeal of tires on the wet pavement created more frightening daydreams. She braced herself for the crash she imagined. Heaped among busted glass and twisted metal, she believed, for certain, that her life would be ended...

This woman's intense and inappropriate fears, called phobias, serve the same purpose as obsessions and compulsions: to divert from deeper fears. *The more energy spent on an irrational fear, the less effort can be directed to your actual source of pain.*

If you are terrorized by such fears, you must search internally for your source of unrest. If you don't, those fears, in some form, will always remain.

Numbing

A living, breathing specter of death stared spookily out at her, as the mirror reflected back her own image. With skin that clung tightly to her bones, and sunken black circles around her eyes, this skeletal image she saw in the mirror reflected what she felt inside. Seeing rotting flesh, impervious to any human feeling, it was her own deadened spirit which appeared to her in the looking glass. Part of her was glad, since she worked hard to become numb and deathlike. She would never have to feel again. But, she wanted to be sure.

As she watched the reflection, her right hand grasped the blade of a knife and held it against her cheek. With the methodical skill of a surgeon, she sliced through her cheek, opening a diagonal slit that all-but cut her cheek in half. However, as she watched the blood flow from the cut, she felt absolutely no pain; the face she saw in the mirror could have belonged to someone else. But still, she wanted to be certain.

She wanted to be assured that she could be her own anesthesiologist. Although she had no control over her father's departure, or whom her mother remarried, she wanted control over her feelings. She wanted to freeze the spring of tears that still flowed even years after her father left. She wanted to stop the bitter taste she had in the back of her throat each time she thought of her stepfather. She wanted to freeze the anger and frustration she felt toward a man who attempted to be a substitute father. To her, he was an unwelcome intruder, whose control over her life, she bitterly resented. She wanted to be numb. With the same startling results, she cut into the soft tissue of her cheek twice more. Now she was satisfied ...

At 13, although this girl did her best to stay numb from her feelings, a part of her knew that her pain still remained within her. During a school project, she wrote the following poem.

Eaten deep by weath'ring nature,
The proud and aging twisted oak
Stood all bent and drooped with pain,
For years had rotted deep the scars
To leave but blackened shadows dim.

The dried old leaves now fell to bruise,
Caused by endless cycling time.
The moss and growth
Crept and covered
The airless seeking bark, 'till death.

Over twenty years later, this woman entered SCT and began to feel her past hurts. Once she allowed them to surface, she was able to start the healing process. With their release she no longer needed to be numb, and she began to feel joy, beauty, and laughter once again.

My feelings are surrounded by a
gray, steel rod.

My feelings are padlocked in a huge
box that resides in the center of my
chest.

I imagine a large dose of Maalox
coating and soothing my stomach,
providing a protective barrier between me and my feelings.

My feelings lie buried under topsoil.

I exist surrounded and functioning in
a clear, but unpiercable cocoon. I can
see the earth but stay untouched by
it. I release no feelings into the world
and absorb no feelings from it.

These descriptive analogies from some of my clients represent the unique ways in which they have used the numbing process to protect themselves from experiencing their aches. With their pain locked deep inside them, the numbing serves to also lock out all pleasure. Until they purge their emotional hurts, these people are like the walking dead.

Multiple Personalities

Softly, he asked me to remove all the pens and pencils from my desk. Pointing to these "weapons," he demanded that I hide them from him. As a result of his therapeutic process, he had become aware of Joe, and was concerned for my safety. Joe was frightening. When he showed up, he took charge; and he was vicious.

Most of the time, he was good at keeping Joe, Shawn, and Phil—the personalities that lived within him—hidden. Expending a good deal of energy on concealing them, he was able to maintain control and play the adult roles in life. On the surface, he appeared strong. This was an image he portrayed, both to himself and to the rest of the world. Overall, he remained emotionally separate from them, only intellectually aware of their existence.

Joe remained hidden, but ready to pounce. Sometimes, with just a harsh tone from a boss, friend, or stranger, Joe would begin to stir, expand with power, and attempt to break through. On those occasions he could feel his face swell with heat and pressure. He could feel Joe growing and pushing his way out. He sensed Joe's efforts to free himself, as he bulged against the walls of his body. Joe wanted to overpower him and crack through the hell of his present image. He knew that if he permitted it, Joe would take total command. Joe would have all the authority and he would be helpless. They would literally change places. Fearing that loss of control, and the consequences of Joe's ferocity, he consistently struggled to keep Joe locked within his body.

Sometimes, he would sense Joe's presence outside of his. Ghost-like, he would stand at the entrance to the bedroom or float within the mirrors of the house. He knew that Joe wanted to possess his body and convert it into an instrument of fury.

Scared of contact with Joe, he did his best to avoid him. Whenever he saw Joe, he would scrunch up his body and tightly close any garment that left parts of him exposed. He would avoid any space which Joe occupied, and, if he had to, would walk quickly around him.

Occasionally, no matter how much he avoided contact with this ghostly figure, or concentrated on containing it under his skin, Joe would emerge. Defeating all efforts to restrain him, Joe would burst out.

Joe made one such appearance at the dinner table. As they ate, his girlfriend began to criticize him. She insisted that he was selfish, insensitive, uncooperative, and manipulative. She complained about his lack of responsibility and commitment toward her. He made a few feeble attempts to defend himself, and it was at this point that Joe became aware of the conversation, from his hiding place.

Shortly, however, his girlfriend became more irritated, and her voice grew angry. Interrupting him, she began to stifle each of his protests. At this juncture, Joe's interest began to peek, and he listened more intently.

When she shouted "you bastard," Joe suddenly energized and leapt into action, as he did each time the man was threatened.

Overcoming any meager restraint he placed in Joe's way, Joe entered his bloodstream and prepared to exert his influence. He began to surge with power, muscling down any portion of gentleness that remained. Vanquished, he lay helplessly beneath Joe's ever expanding force. With each drop of adrenaline that pumped into his newly possessed body, Joe grew larger and stronger. One hundred percent raw, unbridled fury, he felt empowered with a fearless invincibility.

In a voice much deeper than that of the man he now possessed, Joe cursed at the woman. Clearing a path to his target, Joe shoved all the dinner dishes aside. With dazzling speed, he grabbed the utensils in her hand and threw them across the room. With access to the woman now clear, Joe was ready to destroy her.

Shocked and bewildered, the woman had no time to react. Joe moved too quickly. Reaching his vice-like hands to the back of her head, Joe's palm and fingers closed on a clump of hair. Using the hair as a handle, Joe yanked the head forward and smashed the woman's face into the table. Without regard to the scattering and breaking dishes, Joe continued to bash the woman over and over again. His only purpose was to destroy. He feared nothing and the woman presented no challenge ...

To his surprise, he stayed with this woman longer than all the others. Usually, whenever he felt some intimacy or closeness, Shawn would begin to emerge. The threat of commitment would quickly activate Shawn's coldness and his distaste for women. Transforming all feelings of sensitivity and warmth into the passions of disgust and disdain, Shawn would take control of him. To Shawn, any woman was a despicable stranger. He wanted to leave and sever all future ties.

Without any compassion, Shawn would cooly confront the woman that disgusted him, and inform her of his plans to leave. He would explain each detail of his departure, unmoved by the woman's reactions. Her pleas and tears deflected easily off his steel exterior. To him, she was pathetic, weak and useless. Shawn was anxious to be rid of her.

Shawn would then quit his job, pack his belongings, and move to a new community. Acquiring a new home and a new career, he would feel relieved and excitedly free. Soon, Shawn would began to relax and then relinquish command ...

Once acclimated to his new surroundings, Phil would blossom and expose himself to the world. Like a gigolo in the heart of the city, he waited anxiously and somewhat impatiently on the street corners for his next sexual conquest.

Filled with desire, Phil would easily coax a new woman into his life. Then, obsessed with sex, his energy boundless, he took control, holding the woman captive by his desires.

He craved nothing but sex. Food and sleep were annoying distractions. He often lay locked in passion's embrace with his mate, for hours—or even days.

In an attempt to satisfy himself, he would act out all his sexual fantasies, as well as those of his partner. However, no matter in which position they mated, or how long he stayed inside her, Phil remained unsated.

The woman, however, felt different. She was physically satisfied, and she wanted more than just sexual contact. She wanted to bond on many levels with Phil. She sought to touch, stimulate, and merge spirits; not just genitals. She wanted them to share their pasts, mingle in the present, and listen to each other's future aspirations. She wanted to experience the pleasure of a complete relationship.

Phil, however, was not capable of such an experience. He was absolute sexual vigor, and knew of nothing else. He had no past and no interest in the future. He operated only in the dimension of undiluted animal instinct. He was not capable of a whole relationship and felt threatened by the woman's needs.

Whenever Phil's relationships reached such levels of commitment, Shawn's cold demeanor would begin to spread and overcome Phil. Shawn would then dominate and the cycle would continue ...

How did these personalities come into existence? Why did they take residence inside him? From where did they get their strength? What did they want? What was their purpose?

In the beginning of counseling, his conscious resisted all attempts to recall any details surrounding the inception of these personalities. For a long while he withstood the challenge of his subconscious to push the past into focus. Gradually, however, messages and memories from his childhood began to emerge as physical manifestations in his body. He began to feel physical pain and wounds that had been locked inside his cells, sinews, and muscles for over 20 years. Still not consciously aware of specific events, his body began to communicate with his mind.

During a powerful therapy session, his body began to relive some type of physical abuse inflicted upon him many years ago. He recorded this experience in the poem below.

Smaller and Smaller

My eyes hidden from her
I weep but no tears fall
Blow after blow

Beaten blackened limbs
With blood oozing
Shivering
Helpless
Swallowed up
All warmth depleted

Only my bruised body
My bruised spirit remains
Lifeless body
Shamed forever
Feeling smaller
Smaller and smaller
Until I am no more

This man actually felt the physical sensations of the abhorrent physical abuse that he was subjected to as a child. During session, his body relived the trauma, and reacted as it did some 20 years earlier. Turning cold, he felt the warm flames of life's energy being extinguished from his small, delicate being. Helpless, childlike, and victimized by coercive attacks, he could feel his spirit slipping away. His innocent soul, once flowering with potential, lay cold and dead.

As he discovered in SCT, both the death of his natural childlike soul, and the birth of his other identities, had distinct purposes. As a powerless child, in order to escape experiencing the horror, he had to find a way of separating from it. Such evil was just too much to bear. So, he buried the part of him that experienced the abuse. It was a way of surviving such betrayal, and the only kind of control he had. In a strange way, his spiritual death was his escape from horror. Under the circumstances, it was the best diversion possible. However, with his natural self put to rest, he still needed a way to function in the world. Born from the ashes of his emotional destruction, each identity would begin to play its own unique part in his new script for life.

Each personality seemed to embody a strong, but different, emotion that he could not consciously express. Separate and concealed from each other, as well as from his dead and abused self, the one who reigned in the moment felt only its own undiluted emotion. His strong multiple personalities kept him diverted from the past horror.

Involved in SCT, this man is still trying to uncover the soul that lay dormant. He is still attempting to recall all the details to his past misery, and with such recollection render his multiple personalities useless. Once his poisons are felt and released, his other identities will no longer have their roles to play. He can become a whole person, aware of his feelings and no longer in need of diversions. Then, he can direct his energies to nurturing the self that he long ago buried. In a sense, he can be reborn and have a second chance at life.

4

Transference and Projection: More Diversions

Transference

Veiled in the pipe smoke of Freudian mysticism or the psychological jargon of neo-Freudian analysts, the concept of transference is really a simple one and is illustrated by the following case...

Once again, Kenny awoke soaked in his own urine. The shivering caused by the dampness of his pajamas was minimal compared to the trembling he had when he thought about his mother's anger.

Removing the blanket, Kenny rose from the bed and listened intently to the sounds of the house. He was in luck. His mother was not yet awake. He rushed over to his dresser and yanked open the drawers. His hands rifled through the clothes, as his body quaked with fear. He dressed silently and prayed that his mother would not wake.

Tossing his wet pajamas into the hamper, Kenny then covered the moist sheet with his blanket. Though Kenny knew that this attempt was futile, he wanted at least a temporary escape from his mother's wrath. So he grabbed his schoolbag and rushed out the door. Although grateful for the morning reprieve, he knew that the afternoon would approach quickly enough.

Kenny walked to school with his head bent and his shoulders slouched, burdened by a heaviness well beyond his 7 years. Focusing on the ground, Kenny envied the grass and pebbles. They would never have to be called "little baby wetter" in front of friends. Nor would they ever have their faces shoved in their soiled sheets until they gagged from the stench. Rocks and grass never would feel the weight of such shame.

Arriving at school, he looked up at the teacher. She reminded him of his mother. In fact, he believed she knew what happened at night and that she could see the yellow urine stains that covered his sheets. He expected that, just like his mother, she would embarrass him in front of the other children. When she called on him in class, his voice stuttered with panic. He hated her, too. He wished she would die. But, by the end of the day she hadn't scolded or shamed him and he could feel his shoulders straighten and his head lift. Maybe, today, his mother might show some mercy as well.

On his way home, Kenny played with some of his classmates who lived in the neighborhood. But, his fun ended abruptly when he spotted his bedsheets waving like flags in the wind outside his bedroom window. This was another one of his mother's attempts to change him by showing the world that he was a bad boy. Immediately, Kenny felt an ache in his stomach. As this ache spread throughout his body, all feelings of joy disappeared. Kenny could feel his body shrinking. Dwindling with each teasing remark from the other children, his head and shoulders once again drooped downward. Beseeching the grass with his eyes, Kenny begged to vanish into the soil. Absorbed by the blades of grass he could then rest peacefully in the sunshine and never have to feel such pain. However, his fantasy was not to be. Kenny was forced to spend his days in his mother's hellish domain.

Sluggishly, Kenny walked into his house, climbed the stairs to his room, and shut the door. Lying in a fetal-like position on his bed, Kenny tried to avoid all contact with his mother. The more withdrawn and isolated he could stay, the safer he felt.

When contact was unavoidable, Kenny remained quiet, trying not to incite his mother into a further rage. Tightening his stomach muscles, he attempted to hold back the shame, fear, anger, and inadequacy that so tortured his little soul. Sometimes, he visualized loosening the muscles of his belly and vomiting on his mother. Smiling, he would watch the mess stream down her face, just like his tears which so often soaked his pillow at night.

However, Kenny never did confront his mother and "puke back" the feelings that her denigration caused him. Instead, he stuffed them down and removed them from his conscious awareness. As a result, though he matured physically, he retained, deep within him, the painful feelings from his youth. In adulthood, these feelings were consistently re-awakened and reactivated by contact with other women. A brief interchange with a waitress, saleswoman, coworker, or telephone operator caused him to shutter with discomfort. Flirtatious overtures incited a shimmer of disdain, and sometimes just the sight of a woman caused him to cringe with disgust. Feeling smoldering anger in the center of his chest, he sensed his body temperature rise. Attempting to prevent this anger from bursting out, he did his best to shorten all communication with women. However, some connections were impossible to avoid.

In conversations with his female boss, Kenny felt his body hunch and curl up, as he anticipated being scolded. He expected to be admonished for something he did wrong. Feeling trapped, Kenny's stomach tightened as it did when he was a child, and he tried to prevent the shame from exploding like shrapnel throughout his body. Almost at the same instant, Kenny's mind pictured various ways of causing this woman considerable anguish. Trembling and nauseous at the completion of the interchange, Kenny retreated to his office.

Instead of curling up into a fetal ball, as he did in his childhood bedroom, Kenny sought comfort from his water cooler. Drinking the cool water only temporarily quenched the feelings that burned within him.

In reality, most of the women that surrounded Kenny did not wish to embarrass, scold, or humiliate him. His female boss usually sought him out for his professional expertise. However, Kenny's subconscious desired to release the feelings that still burned inside him from his relationship with his mother. But, his conscious mind would not permit him to confront the true source of his pain. So Kenny struck a compromise between his subconscious and conscious by *transferring* his past anger, pain, and mistrust onto all other women. Although this compromise kept Kenny diverted from his past, it had dire consequences in the present; he lived alone, withdrawn, and completely isolated from the opposite sex.

~ ~ ~

As with the concepts of good-evil, right-wrong, love-hate, and black-white, the concept of transference has two extreme, distinct, and equally powerful categories. Each category is an indicator of the type of past feelings and needs that still abide within a person's psyche. Like the poles of a magnet, transference can be either repelling or attracting. In the preceding case, Kenny's transference was of the repelling kind. He transferred unpleasant feelings that lingered within him from his relationship with his mother onto other females and, as a result, he was repulsed by them.

In the popular movie *"Pretty Woman,"* the lead character forges an entire career by transferring his stored fury onto others. Like a vulture, he seeks out dying and floundering businesses and buys them at extremely inexpensive prices. He then proceeds to dismantle them, selling their individual parts for great profits. Making millions, he delights in watching their owners squirm as the remnants of their life's endeavors are picked apart.

As a child, abandoned by his businessman father, this character was left with tremendous rage. Although young and powerless he longed to destroy the man that caused him and his mother so much agony. However, instead of confronting and releasing his anger toward his father—the source—he transferred it onto other businessmen, deriving revengeful pleasure from their suffering.

~ ~ ~

In some instances, when repelling transference is operating with its greatest intensity, the results may be violent and catastrophic ...

As her ears picked up the sound of the short siren burst, the woman's eyes glanced at her rear-view mirror. The red strobe-like effect of the flashing lights was a harsh reminder of the realities of her own life. Instantly, she felt the pressure build inside her abdomen, as the lights seemed to blink in tandem with her own convulsing stomach muscles. Sighing, she steered her car onto the shoulder of the road and gradually slowed to a stop.

Not knowing what she did wrong, she waited for the policeman to approach her car. Resigned to getting a ticket, she watched his black boots in her side mirror. As the boots got closer, she braced herself for another one of life's struggles.

Looking up and into his eyes as he explained the details of her speeding, she searched for some haven of comfort. Bursting into tears, she began an explanation for her lack of concentration on the roadway.

Abandoned by her husband, she felt lost and frightened. Drained by the burden of trying to survive on her own, she found it difficult to concentrate on anything else.

Relating her story, she was relieved and surprised by the policeman's reaction. The wrinkles on his forehead disappeared and his eyes softened. Identifying with her struggles, he began to share as well.

Sharing such common wounds bridged their separate lives and no longer did they feel like strangers. There was a deep understanding between them. In an attempt to enhance their bonding and escape from their daily gloom, they drove to a local hotel.

Sexually aroused by the emotional support they found in each other, they hoped that such pleasure could continue. However, their emotional and carnal delights were short-lived. As the policeman allowed himself to feel close to this woman, he also allowed his intense pain and rage to surface. From his eyes came tears of vulnerability, and out of his mouth came words of hurt. "Karen, how could you just leave? How could you do this to me; to us? You're tearing me apart. Let's try again. I don't want to go on without you. Please don't do this. Please, Karen, please ..."

Puzzled, the woman began to respond. "What are you talking about? I'm not Karen." This time as she looked into his eyes she saw a wild, distant, and painful look. He wasn't with her. He was lost in a different place and time. She began to understand what was happening. Panicking, she pleaded "I'm not Karen. I'm not the one who hurt you." Her words had no effect, as his fists first pounded her stomach and than battered her face. Trembling from the shock and the pain, she tried once more. "Please, I'm not your wife ..." Her pleas were useless. His hands wrapped around her neck and choked her to death.

Although disguised, this situation is based on a recent, true incident. It illustrates an extreme and fatal consequence of intense transference. In this case, the policeman lost his contact with reality and actually believed this woman was his wife. Never effectively resolving and releasing feelings he had toward his wife, he exploded them onto another woman, and tragically caused her death.

In attracting transference an individual is drawn to a person whom they believe can somehow satisfy the needs and wants that were never met by their primary caregivers or (as in this case) other intimates. Like children stuck in their early developmental years, these individuals seek out relationships in which they will be nurtured, comforted, protected, and loved. Although chronologically adults, they continue to search for an ideal guardian; someone who will fill the deep emptiness left within them by others.

~ ~ ~

After his intense involvement in SCT, a man in his late forties became painfully aware of his attracting transference and expressed his thoughts and feelings in the poem below.

Transfer

I transferred on a bus to go across town
and somehow felt I would meet the woman
in the gown.

As a child I hid in her skirt.
I did not want to go out and play in the dirt.

An old woman got on the bus to Central Park
West.

She sat across from me and I immediately put
her to the test.

I looked across the aisle and hoped to God she
would notice me. I said, "Isn't it a nice day?"

She looked at me and turned her head, and I
knew I could not stay.

I ran off the bus at the next stop. I breathed in
deep and said, "Oh God, she wasn't my
mother."

I turned around to get on a bus to search for
another.

One who could make me feel safe and
I would know that I did belong.

I go through life and search for the
quasi mother who is always wrong.

For over 30 years this man's romantic endeavors
were motivated by his attracting transference and thus,
usually ended in disaster. Like a child, he demanded
affection and nurturance, but offered none in return. He
sought an ideal parent, not an ideal lover. Most of the
women he came in contact with desired a healthy,
balanced, and mature relationship. They felt pressured,
drained, and choked by his needs and eventually left
him.

During SCT this man realized that expecting other
women to compensate for his mother's lack of affection
was really an attempt to hide from his childhood

wounds. To unchain himself from the bondage of his transference he had to re-experience this pain from the true source, his mother. Once these feelings were released he no longer had the need to divert by transferring onto other women.

Now, let's take a brief look at some additional examples of both types of transference. First, I have described each client's transference-based reaction. Then I have given the explanation or the original source of this transference.

Repelling Transference

A woman shivers, jumps, and becomes angry when approached from behind.

As a child, this woman's stepfather would poke his index finger in her back while he scolded and lectured her. Following her from room to room, this routine continued for hours.

As she watches her husband read the newspaper, a woman slams her fist onto the dinner table, splattering both food and drink.

During her early years, this person's father would ignore her and continue to read his newspaper for hours.

Approaching my desk to obtain a pencil, a woman recoils in fear.

As a child, this person was forbidden to touch any item that belonged to her mother. Her young hands were slapped whenever they explored her mother's desk, drawers, or jewelry box.

Flustered, frightened, and crying, a man attempts to wipe his spilled coffee from my carpet.

Most of his innocent childhood accidents provoked his father's wrath. Each mishap would result in a beating.

A woman shouts at her husband for taking a day off from work.

During her childhood, this woman's father rarely worked. As he idled away most of his days in the haze of alcohol, she and her mother assumed the emotional, organizational, and financial responsibility for the entire family.

A woman cries and retches after experiencing a sexual orgasm with her husband. She is very confused by such contrasting pain and pleasure.

In addition to the violation she felt from the incestuous relationship she had with her father, she also experienced physical pleasure by being with him.

Seeing his wife file her fingernails as he begins to talk with her, a man furiously storms out of the house, slamming the door as he goes.

This man's mother paid more attention to her own grooming needs than to his childhood needs. He constantly felt ignored and neglected.

Attracting Transference

Each evening a man rides the subway for three hours seeking out elderly women to talk with.

During his childhood, his mother's devotion was spent on his handicapped brother. As the healthy child, he was expected to raise and comfort himself.

Watching the smiling, attentive stewardess during an airline commercial, a young man immediately makes reservations on that carrier.

Throughout his childhood, this individual sought loving contact with his mother. In every instance, he was rejected.

A man steals clothes from the textile company where he works and gives them as gifts to his girlfriends.

As a child, this person would watch his father receive hugs and kisses of appreciation for the female garments he brought home. Feeling unloved by his mother, he was envious.

Each day a man works 4 hours overtime, not for monetary compensation, but for a smile and acknowledgment from his female boss.

As a youngster, this individual received absolutely no praise, recognition, encouragement, or physical affection from his mother.

A mature woman demands that her husband carry her to bed each night, tuck her in, and talk "baby-talk" to her.

Abandoned by her father as a result of a bitter divorce, she felt deprived of all fatherly love.

Dual Transference

Often, a person will use both types of transference within a single interaction. Let's take a look at a possible scenario for such a dual transference.

Dressed in white, indicating her devotion to the ill and afflicted, the nurse peeked out from the reception window and called his name. Hopeful, Lloyd grabbed his hastily scribbled notes and quickly answered her call.

As the doctor's hands glided, probed, and poked his body, he felt lovingly attended to and cared for. With the security he felt from the doctor's touch, Lloyd wanted to stay longer. But that was not possible, since the doctor had to see his other patients.

No longer caressing Lloyd's body, the doctor issued a rapid, professional, and positive diagnosis. Lloyd knew his time was up, but felt abandoned as the doctor exited. Left alone to dress himself, Lloyd's hope vanished. Lloyd became angry that the doctor had failed to attend to him until "a cure was found." Storming out of the office, he concentrated on making another appointment with a different physician. Perhaps the next doctor would be able to help him.

However, no doctor could possibly cure the ailments that afflicted Lloyd's body, and the notes he scribbled in the waiting room made that clear: "Doctor save me ... Doctor, please notice me ... Look at me, Doctor ... Heal me, help me ... Please give me love ... Doctor, Doctor, help me, please ..."

Emotionally wounded by his parents' lack of affection Lloyd's ills were within his heart. Lloyd, at first, transferred his desire for parental love onto each doctor. Attracted to them by the expectation of being nurtured and comforted, Lloyd was consistently frustrated and disappointed. As every doctor performed his professional duties, Lloyd felt dismissed. However, the true source of these feelings of neglect was Lloyd's parents. Not wanting to deal with them, Lloyd then transferred his anger at his parents onto the doctors, and accused them of incompetence.

Our hypothetical Lloyd went from doctor to doctor and remained stuck in an unfulfilling cycle of dual transference. Until he becomes aware of his patterns through SCT, Lloyd will continue to search for parental love from others, and become angry when this quest is not satisfied.

Counter Transference

Frequently, during interchanges between people, one person's transference spawns another person's transference, or as it's commonly called, counter-transference. Let's take a brief look at transference and counter-transference in action.

As he reached for his notebook, Michael's hand grabbed only air. Instantly, feelings from his childhood were uncapped. As if guided by some emotional blueprint from the past, Michael mechanically moved into the kitchen.

Screaming furiously, he shook his wife Sally, who was busy washing the dishes. He wanted to hurt her for her selfishness and lack of consideration. How dare she not return his notebook to its proper place!

Stunned, Sally's eyes opened wide while the rest of her remained paralyzed with fear. In a panic, she held back both her tears and her words.

Summoning just enough strength to leave the kitchen, Sally headed toward the bedroom. Closing the door behind her, she collapsed on the bed. Pulling her knees up toward her chin, Sally grabbed her legs and curled into a little ball. Locked in this position, Sally released her tears, and wept until morning.

As if transported back in time, both Sally and Michael were trapped in a *transference warp*. Something as simple as a missing notebook could bring Michael back to the house in which he spent his youth. Invading his room, Michael's mother moved, displaced, discarded, and stole his belongings at her will. As she ignored his protests, Michael stored his fury with a helpless resignation. In later years, Michael transferred it onto Sally. He did not see, feel, hear, or respond to *Sally*. As if back in childhood, Michael felt and reacted to his *mother*.

Sally, in turn, seemed whisked back to the past as well. As Michael began his scoldings, Sally became intimidated. As if a child once more, she heard her father's words; "You're no damned good, you lousy kid. Get away from me, you moron." Responding to Michael as she did to her father, Sally would first separate, weep all night, and then isolate herself for weeks.

Both our hypothetical Sally and Michael ignore the true sources of their pain, intermittently transferring and counter-transferring on each other, and, as a result, suffering the agonies and emptiness of an unfulfilling present. SCT can help them come to terms with the true sources of their pain and find peace with each other.

~ ~ ~

As with an unwanted heirloom, transference is often passed from one generation to the next. Like vessels filled with toxic residue from their childhood families, parents frequently spill these poisons onto their own children.

Unloved, unappreciated, and unacknowledged during their youth, parents of one of my clients expected her to attend to their daily needs, soothe their pain, and fill their emptiness. Although she cooked, cleaned, washed their clothes, assisted in their grooming, and wiped their tears, it was never enough. Her parents expected continued parenting. As a result, she spent her childhood attending to them and neglecting herself. But, as with the wicked stepsisters of Cinderella, she could never perform enough to satisfy them and they remained miserable.

On her wedding day her parents informed her that they wished to sell their house, car, and furniture so they could move in with her. With the additional income of her husband they also saw no need to keep their checking account. They expected to be clothed, fed and sheltered. When she finally denied these demands they became furious and refused to communicate with her for many months.

Starved for her own nurturance and resentful for her emptiness, she subsequently expects her own children and husband to take care of *her*. When her expectations are not met, or her children shirk their mothering duties, she responds in anger and coldness.

Until such a cycle can be broken by one courageous family member reaching out to SCT, every generation will suffer from the counter-transference of their parent's pain.

Regardless of what type or how it rears its diversionary head, transference is a powerfully effective way to avoid. By convincing ourselves that current individuals are the cause for our discomforts, or that they can fill the voids we feel, our conscious is able to stay detached and unaware of the original, and most intense, source of our pain.

Projection

Reverend Bob Jameson stepped up to the podium and raised his hands in praise of God. His eyes flashed condemnation as he beseeched his congregation to turn away from the wages of sin and embrace the salvation that was theirs in the Lord Jesus Christ.

Moved to tears by the very conviction of their spiritual guide's words, Reverend Jameson's flock began to chant and wave their arms in celebration of the Lord's saving grace.

"Remember my friends," he began in summation, "the Book of Roman's, Chapter 6: Verse 23 tells us, "... the wages of sin is death, but the gift of God is eternal life in Christ Jesus, our Lord."

In the 3 years since Bob Jameson had been placed in charge of this peaceful congregation's salvation, he had condemned the sinfulness of rock 'n roll music, long hair, fornication, adultery, beer and hard liquor, homosexuality, and material wealth. But, as he challenged his members to repent from the sure damnation of such evils, he filled his grand estate with expensive cars, clothes, and jewels.

And tonight, as he had done so many times before, he would troll the "business district" of the neighboring towns in search of satisfaction for his own unquenchable lust. And tomorrow, his own weaknesses would begin to fill the pages of the sermon he would deliver to the good people of his congregation the following Sunday.

Reverend Jameson used each member of his congregation as a sort of blank movie screen. Onto each person he projected his own sins and desires. Such projection of unsavory qualities onto others is truly a powerful diversion. Judging others for what we feel, believe, and often act on is a common escape from the pain of our own pasts.

As with transference, projection may materialize in other forms. Another kind of projection is alleging that *others* feel a certain way about *us* when we really feel that way about ourselves. For example, one of my clients consistently suggested that if other people found out about his homosexuality they would judge him to be weird and abnormal. As he discovered in SCT, a huge part of *himself* felt guilty and ashamed of his own sexuality. *He* was the one who felt different, and was his own convicting judge. As long as he projected those feelings onto others and assumed that they were the condemners, he was able to stay detached from his own sense of shame and never explore its origin. By projecting and focusing on others he was able to divert from himself.

~ ~ ~

A third form of projection is illustrated by the following statements or questions:

How can you eat yogurt? Yuck!

> *How can you want to drive when you can take the train?*
>
> *I can't believe that you would drink your Anisette straight; how could you drink it without black coffee?*
>
> *It's not necessary to go to the baseball game. You can get just as much pleasure from watching it on TV.*
>
> *I can't believe you'd rather have salad instead of sausage.*
>
> *I'm astonished that you would rather go to the amusement park instead of playing in the soccer game.*
>
> *How could you possibly leave the ballgame before the end of the ninth inning?*
>
> *How can you possibly live in those stifling suburbs?*
>
> *You should put on a warm jacket in this weather.*
>
> *How in the world could you have found that movie interesting?*
>
> *Don't go to that restaurant? You'll just hate it!*
>
> *How can you have a baby at your age?*
>
> *Turn the air conditioning on. You'll be more comfortable.*
>
> *Add more color to your picture. It'll look better!*

Such remarks are indicative of the speaker's desire and/or expectations to have others think, feel, and act the way they do. Individuals who project in this manner are attempting to control others into being mirrors or reflections of themselves; they literally want us to be their clones. In my experience, people who consistently project in this way are attempting to create a safe environment for themselves. They believe, "If you're exactly like me, you won't hurt me. You'll feel what I feel, see what I see, and therefore totally accept and understand me." However, if you spend your energy projecting onto and controlling others, you are avoiding the reasons you feel so unsafe, unaccepted, and misunderstood. You are spending your time diverting from your original source of pain, and your deeper emotional hurts.

5
Countering Diversions:
Creating Awareness

So far, in the journey toward emotional well-being, I've explored the myriad of unhealthy methods designed and constructed to keep us hidden from our internal pain. As so often explained, our conscious mind's desire to inhibit knowledge of our true sources, locks our feelings inside and perpetuates a tormenting cycle of diversions.

The initial phase of Awareness is crucial to unlocking our internal discomforts and beginning the true healing process. However, uncovering buried memories and experiences is no easy task. Although the mental health community frequently touts *awareness* as "the first step toward growth and healing," it does not, as readily, describe how to attain such awareness. As with each step of SCT, the process of achieving increased awareness requires concentration, courage, and commitment.

Awareness, according to SCT, means recalling significant events in your life, getting in touch with the feelings associated with these events, and recognizing the impact of such feelings. This requires the effort to take a good hard look at yourself. Some of the material I have presented thus far may have already triggered your process of introspection. You can further this process of self-examination by using some of the techniques I've touched upon in previous chapters as well as those I'll introduce now. At times, during your trek toward emotional health, you may find it helpful to consult and work with a professional therapist.

Language of Awareness

As explored in the first few sections of Chapter 3, the manner in which we communicate can perpetuate our lack of awareness and denial of feelings.

To facilitate awareness, you must make a concentrated effort to think and speak in the first person. Making broad, general statements about all human beings or the universe as a whole, when you are really referring to yourself, is a way to stay unaware. Speaking in the first person will assist you in experiencing the feelings connected with your thoughts and statements. As a result, your self-awareness will be heightened. In addition, try to avoid other expressions which create denial or lack of ownership for your feelings. Statements or phrases that begin with "maybe," "perhaps," "if," "probably," "I guess," enhance your vagueness rather than your awareness.

The following chart illustrates some of the do's and don'ts regarding the language of awareness.

Using Language of Awareness

Use the first person
   Avoid other pronouns such as *you, we, they, everybody, people.*
Do Say ...
   I really want to have a chid. I'm afraid that I'd miss an experience in life that's very important to me.
Don't Say ...
   Most women want children. They say you miss something in life without them.

Avoid the pronoun "it."
Do Say ...
    I'm so frustrated with my parents for not
      understanding and accepting my feelings.
Don't Say ...
    It can be frustrating for people if they can't get
      their parents to understand.

Use direct, precise, clear statements.
    Avoid words or phrases like *"I think ...," "I*
      guess ...," "Probably ...," "You know ...,"
      "It seems ..."
Do Say ...
    I was really hurt when my husband left me. I
      felt so lonely.
Don't Say ...
    I guess it hurts you when someone you know
      leaves. It seems kind of empty when a
      person is alone.

Focusing on diversionary behaviors is another effective way to enhance your self-awareness. As examined in Chapters 3 and 4, a behavior may be diversionary based on its intensity, frequency, and duration. Behaviors that evoke inappropriate intensity, that occur very often, and that have been occurring for a long period of time are those to be explored. If necessary, refer back to Chapters 3 and 4 for the kinds of behaviors that warrant examination.

Once you have determined one or more of your diversionary behaviors, begin to explore them by asking yourself some key open questions. An open question is designed to elicit more than just a yes or no response. Its focus is to evoke self-exploration and asks you to deeply examine thoughts and feelings. Open questions begin with the words "what," "how," and "where," rather than "do you," "are you," and "will you." Such open questions will help you uncover the true purpose of your diversionary behavior. Let's take a look at some examples of this effective questioning method.

Behavior:
Smiling, laughing, and/or joking while in pain
Open Questions:
What am I trying to hide with my smile?
How do I really feel?
What am I diverting from?

Behavior:
Constant and intense criticism of others
Open Questions:
What does criticizing others do for me?
How do I feel when I criticize others?
What does blaming others do for me?
What's my purpose?
Where does that keep me?
Who am I really criticizing?

Behavior:
Constant and intense anger towards others
Open Questions:
Where does my intense anger come from?
What does it do for me?
What purpose does it serve?
What and who am I really angry at?

Behavior:
Addictions (smoking, drinking, gambling, drugs, etc...)
Open Questions:
What does my addiction do for me?
What am I masking behind my addiction?
How do I feel before I engage in my addiction?
How do I feel after I have engaged in my addiction?
What don't I want to feel?

Behavior:
>Phobic reactions (fear of elevators, heights, insects, contamination, flying, darkness, etc ...)

Open Questions:
>What does my phobia do for me?
>
>How does focusing on my phobia hide my deeper fears or pain?
>
>Where does my deeper pain come from?

Behavior:
>Numbing yourself and withdrawing from others

Open Questions:
>What does numbing and withdrawing do for me?
>
>What does it protect me from?
>
>What makes it difficult for me to connect with others?

Behavior:
>Repelling transference towards another person

Open Questions:
>How do I feel about this person?
>
>What are my reactions when I'm with this person?
>
>Where do these reactions come from?
>
>What or who do I really want to avoid?

Behavior:
>Attracting transference towards another person

Open Questions:
>What makes this person attractive to me?
>
>What emptiness am I trying to fill?
>
>Where did this emptiness come from?
>
>Whose love do I really want?

Behavior:
>Projecting the qualities that you don't like about yourself onto others

Open Questions:
Who really exhibits this quality?
What does this projection do for me?
How did I develop this quality?

Behavior:
Projecting to control others

Open Questions:
Why do I want others to be like me?
What does that do for me?

Remember: As you attempt to answer your questions, use the language of awareness and talk to yourself in the first person.

Dreams

During sleep, while our conscious mind lays at rest, our subconscious is busily at work, attempting to communicate with us through the images of dreams. Taking advantage of the night, it attempts to push into our awareness the unresolved feelings and memories that we keep hidden during the light of day.

Although at rest, our vigilant conscious still acts as a guardian from pain and often attempts to distort what our subconscious is trying to tell us. On first scrutiny, as a result of this distortion, the images and messages in our dreams may seem confusing, nonsensical, fragmented and disjointed. However, like an archaeologist who pieces together bones, fossils, and layers of sediment to gain a picture of the earth's past history, we can analyze the images and fragments of our dreams to acquire a clear representation of our own past background. With effective interpretation of dreams we are able to put into precise focus what still lies buried within us. Let's explore how to accomplish this.

~ ~ ~

"The wheels of the roller-coaster clacked against the tracks as it reached the peak of its ascent. While the car whooshed downward, I heard the people begin to scream with excitement. The wind from the coaster beat against my face and I stood alone at the top of the ride. All sense of amusement rushed from my body and was replaced by an expanding fear. Almost immediately, I had this sense of impending doom.

"As my feet straddled the tracks, I glanced downward and focused on the man wearing the plaid shirt. Horrified, I watched him begin to murder other men who lined the tracks below me. Holding a metal spear in both hands, he would thrust it into the stomach of each person who stood in his way. With each penetration I witnessed, my own body winced with pain. Like a sport fisherman, running the spear completely through the victim, he would then lift them up by the handle of his weapon and drop them over the side of the tracks. With each killing he moved closer to his final goal, which I knew was me.

"Maniacally smiling, he looked up towards me, and, although he whispered the words, I heard them clearly; "Now, I'm coming after you!" Nauseous, shivering, and feeling so helpless, I remained at the top of this fun-ride and anxiously waited for my death ..."

In my experience, one of the most productive methods of creating more awareness through dreams is to view each significant person, place, and thing in the dream as a representative part of yourself. By exploring the above dream in such a manner, this person can piece together its puzzling parts and gain more insight into the pain within himself.

"The people being slain on the tracks were really parts of me which I feel have been wounded, betrayed, and ultimately destroyed throughout my life. Killing my childhood innocence and the sweet part of me that viewed life with a laughing awe, my physically and verbally abusive mother was my first murderer. Teachers, bosses, and other women continued to stab and ruin my creative, free-spirited, and trusting parts. With so many parts of me gone, and so much potential unrealized, I often feel frightened, alone and vulnerable to the cruelty of the world; just like I felt at the top of the tracks.

"The homicidal maniac in my dream not only represented others who have wounded me, but a rageful and bitter part of myself as well. It was this part of me who often killed off decent relationships as well as career opportunities. Indeed, the plaid shirt on the man in the dream depicted all the crossroads and opportunities that I had a hand in destroying. My life has been a treacherous roller-coaster ride, in which many parts of me have died. Some of the treachery has been committed by others, and some by my own spears."

Now, take a look at some additional examples:

"The castle stood ready for an oncoming assault. Through each window, door and any minor opening protruded major weapons of war. Machine guns, cannons, mortars, rifles, and pistols pointed their barrels outward and were prepared to fire. The castle was defended on all sides ...

"When I interpreted the castle as representative of myself, the dream made total sense to me, and I realized how much hurt and anger I still stored inside. Rejected by my cold mother, criticized by my judgemental father, I viewed life as a battleground. Trusting no one, I stayed cautious, withdrawn, and always ready for a fight. Up until this very day, I allow no human intimacy to penetrate the protective defenses which I have erected."

~ ~ ~

"As I drove, the little people laughed and frolicked. Ignoring my pleas for them to restrain themselves, they continually jumped back and forth on the seats of my car. They didn't really look like children, but like squashed adults. Feeling helpless to control such wild and free behavior, I became concerned ...

"Exploring these squashed people as parts of me, I became aware of how much I repressed the fun parts of myself and allowed no time for playful pleasure; I squashed all such desires. Starting at age 5, with my mother busily involved in her work, I had the responsibility of caring for my infant sister. Such duties left little time for romping. Life to me was always serious and free-spirited childhood activities were omitted. I now realize how much I resent being so deprived."

~ ~ ~

"Walking into the bedroom, my eyes were drawn to the two sculptured clay heads that rested on the shelf. One was smiling and the other grimacing in pain.

"Curious, I attempted to discover their purpose, and moved close to them. Almost instantly, as my hands began to search their surface, a swarm of disgusting snakes squiggled, squirmed, and poured out from their eyes, ears, and mouths. Turning my head, I wanted to get away from them as fast as possible. They were just too ugly. They had black, slimy bodies and darting forked tongues.

"Frantically, I ran out of the room and sought help from my mother. However, there was nothing she could do. The snakes had spread throughout the house. Infesting every room, they slithered, slimed and crawled along the walls and ceilings ...

"The heads were truly symbolic of me. I go through life purely acting. I play just the parts and roles of mother, lover, and worker. Nothing ever seems real, solid, or whole. I don't know who I am, and continually put on facades to function in the world.

"You see, inside of me, really lies the truth. Deep in my body squirms an evil ugliness which I still don't want to look at. Just like the snakes in the dream. It's such a crawling horror that it infects and infests my very soul.

"My childhood was filled with tortuous torment. As I tried to comfort my needy, dependent, and controlling mother, my father would consistently satisfy his own sexual needs by taking advantage of my young body. As I did in the dream, I tried to turn away from such malevolence and separate from it. However, I now realize it stayed within me, and to be free, I must clean it out."

~ ~ ~

"Terrified, my mouth was dry and my legs were trembling. Taking two steps at a time, I rapidly ran down the darkened, spiral staircase of the old haunted mansion. But it still followed me, and I could hear its growl-like breathing. No matter how fast I moved the stalking monster kept up with me.

"Reaching the bottom of the stairs, I decided to make a stand against this creature. Turning around, I stuck out my tongue, placed my thumbs in my ears and waved at it with my hands. Undaunted by my act of defiance, the monster answered me back with a deafening roar that chillingly penetrated my spine. I was never so scared in my life ...

"The haunted mansion told me of my own dark, shallow, and empty insides. The monster chasing me is a part of me which I still fear exploring. It's a part of me that I want to run away from; it's cruel, angry, insensitive, and dishonest. It's the part of me that abandoned my brother in his terminal illness when he needed me the most, and consistently betrayed a whole host of human beings. I know now that trying to ignore this part of me certainly won't make it go away."

~ ~ ~

"Standing deep in Sherwood Forest is Maid Marion. She is about 21 years old, and wearing an elegant white gown. She's beautiful, but I sense, somehow, she is lost.

"Robin Hood, carrying a sword in his right hand, emerges through the dense trees. As he approaches Maid Marion, I can tell by his eyes and scowling face that he is angry. I'm afraid for her and feel helpless to stop what I fear is going to happen.

"With his sword, he slices off both her feet at the ankles. Next he cuts off both her arms at the shoulders. As she falls to the ground and lies there powerless, he makes one deep cut in her face from the top of her forehead to the bottom of her chin. I keep staring at her and realize that her beauty is ruined forever.

"Next, he points his sword at her heart. Terrified, she speaks for the first time. 'Please, not that,' she begs. He then rams the sword into her chest and takes out her heart. As she lies there motionless, all I focus on is how her face and body have been brutally marred. Robin Hood then just leaves ...

"The clues in this dream are helping me piece together the puzzle of my buried past. I know that the beautiful Maid Marion in the dream was me. Although I still can't remember all the specific details I know now that my father was responsible for defiling my pure, bright, and silky innocence- with his dark and incestuous evil. I feel so betrayed ..."

Body Language

The effects of stored stress on our human bodies has been well researched, documented and acknowledged.

Stashed tension has been proved to gnaw away at our internal organs causing such ailments as headaches, backaches, muscle tightness, gastrointestinal discomforts, and high blood pressure. Some current research has even pointed to stress as a factor in arthritis, heart disease and cancer. So, stuffed feelings not only result in torturous diversionary behavior, but may take a physical toll on us as well. When that occurs we often panic, scramble to doctors, seek out remedies in an effort to quiet the shouting of our bodies. However, by that time it may be too late to reverse the physical damage. We would be wise to listen to the subtle whispers, clues and messages our body is saying long *before* hidden feelings cause us injury.

As with dreams, in its effort to release unresolved feelings, our subconscious is trying to penetrate our stubborn conscious by communicating through our bodies. Through the subtle dialogue of our body we can achieve tremendous cognizance of what lies within us.

~ ~ ~

Each Saturday morning for the last three years, 34-year-old Mark awoke with a choking lump in his throat and his legs trembling uncontrollably. Visitations to doctors proved fruitless and frustrating, since they could find no physical reasons for his Saturday morning afflictions. Deciding "it was time to get to the bottom of this," Mark entered SCT and began his journey into awareness ...

It was Saturday morning and the chattering of the birds served as little Mark's alarm clock. His tiny legs shook with anticipation as his father walked into the room.

Reaching out his hand, Mark's dad signaled that it was time for their weekly walk. As Mark's little fingers were swallowed up by the strength and size of his father's hand, he felt enveloped with love. Hand in hand they marched off to the corner coffee shop for their special Saturday breakfast.

He loved the shop and felt so comfortable there. It was one of those homey little luncheonettes that peppered the streets of New York. When they arrived Mark knew that they would be warmly welcomed by the owner and the regular customers. Mark loved the attention and was proud to be with his father.

As soon as they opened the door the lovely smell of frying bacon filled Mark's head. Immediately, he dashed to the counter where he could see the cook at work. Swivelling the top of the anchored stool to get a clear view of the grill, Mark watched the eggs bubble and the bacon shrink. That made him hungry.

Today was the only day of the week he could eat anything he wanted. So, he always chose to start with his favorite, a vanilla milk shake. The owner would pour the ingredients in a wide-mouth chrome cup and place it under a huge green and silver mixer. As the blades whirred, Mark wet his lips in anticipation. When the blending was complete, the owner placed a glass on the counter and poured in the delicious mixture from the cup. Since the blending cup held more than the glass, the owner left the extra for Mark to enjoy. Beaming, Mark knew that he would be able to polish off exactly $2\frac{1}{2}$ glasses of this luscious drink. Saturdays were truly special. Mark had everything he could want; his loving father, his favorite drink, and a lifetime of fun to look forward to.

When Mark was 10 years old, his father died unexpectedly from a heart attack. Special Saturday breakfasts were no more, and Mark's sweet world was shattered. After the death of his father, the singing of the birds never seemed to reach his ears ...

At age 34, when Mark sought the source for his trembling legs and knotted throat, I asked him to listen closely to his body. As I asked him "What are your legs and throat saying?—What are they trying to tell you?" Mark began to hear the messages clearly.

"When my dad died I saw how crushed my mother and sister were. I tried to be strong for them. I cried just a trickle at the funeral, and did my best to keep back my tears and be a comfort for them. I now realize that I never gave myself the opportunity to grieve for my dad. Although I missed him terribly, I never allowed my tears to flow. So, as each Saturday, the day of the week I spent with my father, approached, my tears would accumulate as this ball in the back of my throat. My shaking legs spoke of their desire for the Saturday morning breakfast walk, and their inability to make such past pleasures possible. I know now that I must deal with the loss of my father, which occurred over 20 years ago."

Mark listened to his subconscious through the messages he received in his body. Becoming aware of the hurts he never grieved, Mark allowed himself to purge his stored tears, and fully mourn the death of his father. Although still pleased by the fond memories he has of his dad, Mark's legs no longer shake and the lump in his throat is gone. Best of all, according to Mark, "I once again hear the sweet singing of the birds."

If your body consistently exhibits movements or gestures that go beyond its normal functioning needs, talk to it. Ask the parts what they're saying. Although you may not get immediate answers, perseverance will certainly increase your chances of gaining additional awareness, as illustrated by Mark and the examples below.

~ ~ ~

Suffering from a tormenting itch, recurring every few months for the past 10 years, one woman would claw, rip, and scratch at her skin in an attempt to relieve the unbearable irritation. At times, a case of red hives would burst out on her skin and cover most of her body. Medical doctors labeled the condition as eczema and treated it with salves. I implored her to look *under the skin* for her source of misery and to ask herself "What is my skin saying?"

Although resistant at first, she gradually began to hear the messages loud and clear: "My father's touch was so abusive, incestuous, and repulsive, it was as if he left toxic poisons within my system. Since I never released such poisons by dealing with my feelings toward my father they would 'pop out' every so often, on the surface of my skin."

~ ~ ~

During each of her sessions, another woman would constantly shake one of her crossed legs. Although I asked her what it said, she responded by continually claiming that she was just nervous about work, money, and boyfriends. However, after a few months, my questions elicited quite a different answer.

"My leg is really saying that it wants to kick you and all men. The whole bunch of you are no damn good. You just take what you want, use who you want without considering the damage, and then just leave. Just like my father. I hate all of you! I now realize how much rage I've kept inside."

As her head spasmodically jerked, pounding the back cushion of the chair, I asked what it was saying. Her tears and high pitched screams joined the discussion. "I remember clearly how my father's hands forced my head onto his penis. Easily overpowered, my screams were always muffled by the fullness in my mouth."

~ ~ ~

Entering the office, another client would fold both his arms across his chest, sit, and stare at me for the first few moments of his session. When he examined his body language, he heard clearly what it said. "I want to protect myself with the shield of my arms. I want to be safe. I want no one to see how vulnerable I really am. I'm just so used to getting hurt. My own father did nothing but scold and punish me, while my mother rejected any attempts at affection."

6

The Three R's:
Reliving, Re-experiencing,
and Releasing

With increased awareness and understanding of the connections between your present symptoms and your past emotional wounds, you are now prepared to enter the second step of SCT. This phase will require you to relive and re-experience painful events in vivid detail. Past sights, sounds, smells, bodily sensations, and emotions will actually be experienced in the present moment. Take a look at the following example of reliving, which occurred in my office.

"Trying to escape the loud music that's blaring in the living room, I've climbed the stairs to my room. Shutting the door, I feel somewhat relieved from this forced family gathering that my parents so frequently like to have.

"Stretched out on my bed, I lift my head off the pillow and respond to the knock on my door, shouting 'Come in.'

"Uncle Nick is smiling as he stands at the doorway. Reaching into his pocket he says, 'I have a surprise for you,' and pulls out a box of spearmint Chicklets. They're my favorite. Peeling away the fresh cellophane, he pours out four pieces of gum into his palm, and moves closer to me. Now, on the bed, he playfully tells me to open my mouth and close my eyes. His voice sounds deeper than usual. One at a time, he places the pieces of gum onto my lips.

"Uncle Nick's face is touching mine and I can smell his Old Spice shaving lotion. His beard is rubbing against my face and I can feel my cheeks getting sore. I'm frightened and confused. I love Uncle Nick. What's he doing?

"I feel his hand on my right knee, moving upward. Nick's tongue is now licking my shoulder and I can feel his hot smelly beer breath on my neck. I want to scream, but nothing comes out. Both his hands are now touching my breasts and my 11-year-old body feels tiny and helpless next to his. I'm getting sick ..."

Then she threw up in my office.

~ ~ ~

I was also a witness to the following reliving experience:

"Ow! Ow! Ouch! Mommy, please ... please don't hit me!" His arms waved about in a futile attempt to shield himself from the blows. While his body convulsed, his head jerked sideways as her slaps appeared to hit their mark. "Please, Mommy, I'm sorry." With those words the beating seemed to be over.

Then this client began to sob. I watched him close his eyes and grab the pillow from my office chair. Tightly hugging it to his chest, he rocked his body back and forth and was gradually able to calm himself. Yawning, he actually placed his thumb in his mouth, began sucking, and fell asleep, just like he did in his childhood.

Receiving many beatings during his childhood, this 42-year-old man actually relived the above assault in my office. This particular beating was, as he described, "for not wiping my feet and tracking mud into the house."

Reliving the experience, along with many others, this client was able to bring to the surface and cleanse out the horror that was for so long a part of him.

~ ~ ~

Some of you many find it difficult to relive an experience with the intensity or accuracy of the above people. Details, at first, might be vague and your pain might be too strong to stay with for very long. However, the important concept to remember is that any amount of time spent reliving is productive. Even slight amounts of re-experiencing will help release trapped memories and feelings, thereby putting you on the path to healing. Obviously, the more accurate you are in your recollections and the longer you can stay with your pain, the greater will be your release. You may find the skills of self-hypnosis helpful in either beginning your reliving or increasing the intensity of your re-experiencing.

As used here, hypnosis alludes to an experience that is similar to daydreaming. Through relaxation techniques you create a state of mind in which you become more aware of your inner world than your external one. However, unlike daydreaming, hypnosis requires a more goal-directed use of your imagination and there is a purpose to your visualizations.

At first, many people are uncomfortable with the idea of using hypnosis. They often associate it with John Barrymore's portrayal of Svengali, the wicked hypnotist who seduced young and virtuous women to commit his crimes. Such portrayals, where "victims" are "powerless" and under a "trancelike spell" are nonsense and have given hypnosis a negative connotation. Hypnosis is not sleep nor is it a trance. You are never "out of it," nor do you lose control. I like to compare hypnosis to the alternative state of mind that occurs when you're involved in a good book or movie. You're temporarily oblivious to the world around you. You might not be aware of the telephone ringing, the sound of a passing airplane, or someone attempting to speak with you. You are so relaxed and involved in your inner thoughts that many of these distractions go unnoticed. However, you can always reenter your normal state of thinking any-time you wish. You always possess control. If there is an emergency, if you suddenly remember something im-portant you need to do, or if you just choose to, you can always reenter the world of your external reality. The same concept applies to hypnosis. There is simply no evidence in any documented data to justify the fear that people are "out of it" when involved in hypnosis.

Another commonly held misconception is that you may get in touch with emotions that you can not handle. Your conscious mind will not allow that. You will only confront memories of painful issues when and if you are ready to deal with them. Since you are always in control, you can end your experience anytime you choose. So, if you begin to feel overwhelmed with more pain than you are ready to face, you simply reenter your ordinary state of being. You possess the total power to enter or leave a state of hypnosis.

Connected to the above fear is the concern that you won't be able to exit the hypnotic state. From the millions of people who have entered the state of hypno-sis there is not a single case of someone remaining stuck in it. Occasionally, people may move from hypnosis into sleep. The sleep is natural and the awakening normal. Whether you are using self-hypnosis or working with the aid of a therapist, you can and will always come out of it at your own choosing.

Some people claim that they lack the imagination to use hypnosis. If you can daydream, then you can use hypnosis. If you can describe your living room from memory, explaining the colors, furniture, location of windows, etc., then you are capable of using hypnosis.

Many people believe that the ritualistic inductions they see in movies and stage acts are required to enter the state of hypnosis. However, swinging pendulums, arm levitations, special verbal formulas, incantations, music, or other special effects are not necessary. You just have to make the transition from the ordinary way you use your mind to the alternative way required for hypnosis. I have found a technique that works for many individuals. If you choose, you can adapt it to your own liking or simply create your own.

I have divided the hypnotic process into the four steps of natural rhythmic breathing, body relaxation, inner-mind imagery and reentry. You can engage in these steps yourself or you may wish to enlist the aid of a therapist.

Natural rhythmic breathing allows your body to find its own, comfortable rhythm for breathing, creating a state of calmness and tranquility. This facilitates your entry into the second step, body relaxation. Working simultaneously with rhythmic breathing, body relaxation assists you in the relaxation of your muscles. With the calmness induced by both steps, you are then open to imagine and visualize. The third step of inner-mind imagery makes use of your imagination to create mental pictures. When operating at its best, such imagery engages all your senses in a total mind and body experience as you feel, see, hear, and taste the images in your mind. Lastly, reentry is the reversal from inner-mind reality to external reality. It is a gradual way of leaving the visualizations of your imagination and, once again, joining the familiar world.

The following self-hypnosis "script" has been designed to facilitate the reliving experience and is adapted from my book *Sexual Joy Through Self-Hypnosis*, coauthored by Daniel L. Araoz. This script incorporates all four steps of the process and is similar to what many of my clients use to assist them in their reliving experiences.

You might find it helpful to record the script onto a cassette tape so it's available to play back whenever you wish. Or, you might want to ask someone with a soothing voice to record it for you. With practice, the process will become so familiar that you will be able to "play" the script in your own mind without the need for the tape. Eventually, you may become so skilled that you can shorten the breathing and relaxing stage and move quickly into your imageries. Feel free to adapt this script to your own pace and taste.

A Script for
Reliving Childhood Experiences

Natural Rhythmic Breathing

Close your eyes and let your body breathe ... Focus on your body's natural breathing rhythm... Concentrate only on your breathing ... Keep all other thoughts away ... Allow distracting thoughts to easily float out of your mind ... See them fade away as a ship disappears into the horizon... With each breath feel yourself becoming more and more relaxed... Inhale ... Exhale ... Inhale ... Exhale ... That's it ... Now, with each breath imagine your body breathing in air filled with comfort, calmness and relaxation ... Breathe out air filled with tension ... Breathe in relaxation ... Breathe out tension ... Continue breathing in this manner for a minute or so ...

Body Relaxation

Now start to relax your muscles ... Allow the muscles of your right foot to become relaxed ... With each breath you take you feel your foot becoming loose, comfortable, and relaxed ... Allow the relaxation to spread to your right calf ... Your right calf is becoming warm, heavy, and relaxed ... The warmth is spreading to your right thigh ... Your right leg is totally relaxed ... Concentrate on the good, warm feeling in your right leg ... Breathe in relaxation ... Breathe out tension ... Now relax your left foot ... Feel the peaceful relaxation fill your left foot ... Allow the relaxation to spread to your left calf ... That's it ... Allow the relaxation to spread up to your left thigh ... Your left leg is totally relaxed, warm, and heavy ... Concentrate on the good feeling of relaxation in your legs ... Your legs feel loose and so relaxed ... Enjoy the feelings of relaxation in your legs for a moment ...

Now let the relaxation spread through your buttocks and pelvic area ... They feel comfortable ... Breathe in relaxation ... Breathe out tension ... Your buttocks are melting into a state of total relaxation ... Concentrate on the relaxation in your legs, buttocks, and pelvic area ...

You can feel your waist and abdomen become more and more relaxed ... With each breath your waist and abdomen are getting heavier and more relaxed ... Breathe in relaxation ... Breathe out tension ... Now the deep feeling of relaxation moves slowly to your back ... Every muscle in your back is becoming very relaxed, at ease, loose, and wonderfully comfortable ... Every breath increases the relaxation even more ... Concentrate on the deep feelings of relaxation in your legs and the upper part of your body ...

Allow the calmness of relaxation to drift into your right hand ... Your right hand is very relaxed and limp ... Warmth flows up from your right hand into your right arm ... Now your arm is very relaxed, like a rag doll ... Concentrate on the loose, warm, relaxed feelings in your right hand ... Now allow your left hand to grow more and more relaxed ... Your hand is limp and relaxed ... Warm feelings spread through your fingers and hand ...

Warmth and heaviness spread up from your left hand into your left arm ... Feel the relaxed sensations in your left arm ... Focus on the loose and relaxed feelings in your feet, legs, pelvis, abdomen, and arms ... You are so relaxed ... With each breath you take, your body sinks into a deeper state of relaxation ... That's it ... Enjoy the peaceful calmness spreading through your body ... Now relax your neck and shoulders ... Imagine magical and gentle hands massaging away tension with each breath you take ... You're so relaxed and comfortable ... You feel as if great weights have been lifted from your shoulders ... They are warm, loose, and relaxed ... Concentrate on the gentle massaging of your neck and shoulders ... Breathe in relaxation ... Breathe out tension ... Inhale ... Exhale ... Inhale ... Exhale ... Now open your mouth slightly and let the muscles of your mouth relax ... That's it ... All the muscles around your mouth are deeply relaxed ... Your tongue and mouth muscles are very relaxed ... Your jaw is loose and your teeth are not touching each other ... Relaxation spreads through your entire face ... Your eyes feel as if they are gently floating in their sockets ... More relaxed with each new breath of air ... Your eyelids are heavy and relaxed ... Tension is draining out of your face ... Your temples and forehead are so relaxed ... Feelings of relaxation are filling every part of your body from your head to your toes ... It's as if relaxation is flowing through your bloodstream ... Breathe in relaxation ... Breathe out tension ... Your entire body feels wonderfully relaxed ... Enjoy the warmth, heaviness, and relaxation of your entire body.

Inner-Mind Imagery

Now you find yourself at the top of a staircase with ten steps ... The staircase leads down to a wonderful, enjoyable place ... A place where you can be totally at peace ... Perhaps you've been there before ... It's a safe, beautiful place ... As you walk down the steps you get closer and closer to that beautiful place ... You walk down step ten ... You're so relaxed ... Inhale ... Exhale ... Now you're on step nine ... With each step you grow more and more relaxed ... Step eight brings you closer to your beautiful place ... Inhale ... Exhale ... You now walk down steps seven and six ... You begin to see your beautiful place more clearly ... You can feel how relaxed and peaceful you are ... Walk down step five ... Inhale ... Exhale ... You are getting deeper and deeper into relaxation ... Walk down step four ... Step three ... Now step two ... Now step one ... You are in your beautiful place ... You feel so calm and peaceful ... You are soothed by the beauty and the gentleness of your special place ... Look around ... Be aware of what you see ... Be aware of the smells ... Be aware of the sensations ... Listen to the sounds ... Allow yourself the pleasure of feeling ... Notice all the details of your surroundings ... You feel fabulous, calm, and secure ... Inhale ... Exhale ... Enjoy the comfort of your beautiful place for a moment ...

Now imagine that you come to a door ... Going through the doorway will take you back in time ... Back to a time in your childhood ... A particular time or event in your childhood ... As you approach this door you get closer and closer to that time ... You're at the entrance to the door ... You're still relaxed ... Inhale ... Exhale ... You open the door ... Step through the doorway ... Breathe in relaxation ... Breathe out tension ... Now you're back in time ... Explore what you see ... Take notice of the smells ... Be aware of the sensations ... Listen to the sounds ... Allow yourself to experience the feelings ... Stay with them ... That's it ... Continue to experience this time in your childhood for a few more minutes ...

Reentry

Now visualize that door once again ... See yourself turn around and approach it ... As you move closer to the door your childhood fades farther and farther away ... Open the door and pass through it ... As you close the door you will leave that time in your childhood behind you ... You are back in your beautiful, wonderful place ... Peaceful feelings are flowing through you ... You feel relaxed ... Breathe in relaxation ... Breathe out tension ... Take a moment to enjoy this special place once again.

Now, slowly you will walk back up the stairs ... Very slowly ... With each step you take get closer to your ordinary state of mind ... When you reach step ten, you'll feel relaxed but very alert and full of energy ... Now slowly you start to ascend ... Take step one ... You are coming back ... Walk up step two ... Now step three ... You are feeling relaxed but more alert ... Walk up step four and five ... Inhale ... Exhale ... You are getting closer and closer to your ordinary state of mind ... Take step six ... Now you move up step seven ... Now up step eight ... You are ending your journey ... Just a few more steps and you'll be totally alert and awake ... Go up step nine ... Inhale ... Exhale ... You're at step ten and you can open your eyes ... Just take a minute or so to adjust to your surroundings.

~ ~ ~

Before attempting the above self-hypnosis script please keep in mind the following:
1. This is a skill to be learned. As with any skill, the more you practice, the easier it becomes.
2. Don't expect dramatic results at first.
3. You may feel more comfortable making your first attempts with the help of a therapist.

4. Choose an environment that is conducive to self-hypnosis. It should be relatively free from distracting noises or harsh lighting. Soft music may enhance your comfort.
5. Wear comfortable clothing.
6. Sit, rather than lie down. Sitting prevents you from falling asleep and helps you stay more focused on the process. It also gives you the message that you are in total control.
7. Continue your relaxed, natural rhythmic breathing throughout the process. If, at any time, you feel distracted or tense, or if you find your reliving overwhelming, keep breathing. You can also go back to your special place and recapture your serenity. Keep in mind, however, that the longer you can stay with your imagery, the more effective your release.
8. Don't force results. If you're having great difficulty you can go right to the reentry step, and try again at another time. You might find it effective to ask yourself some open questions: What makes this so difficult for me? Where is my resistance coming from? What am I so afraid of? How can I work through my difficulty?

Sometimes, even during self-hypnosis, our conscious will remain powerfully resistant to recalling the specific details of our intense pain. When such restraints operate during hypnosis clues from our past may flow to us in the form of images and symbols, similar to what we experience in dreams. Exploration of such visualizations can also be extremely productive. The following visualizations took form during client counseling sessions.

"I know something's blocking me ... preventing me from feeling ... I see this barrier as an iron cage surrounding my body, and keeping my anger in ... I can see the anger. It looks like black tar beginning to ooze out between the bars ... The rage wants to come out; I've just kept it inside for so long ... Now, the tar has transformed into a Frankenstein-like monster ... It wants to kill, destroy ... It's ferocious and monstrous ... I sense that this monster is my own rage toward my father ... I want to crush him, smash him, yet I desperately want him to hold me, hug me, touch me, love me ... I'm angry and I'm hurt at the same time ..."

~ ~ ~

"I'm now in a forest, and—in the distance—I see a blonde woman walking away from me ... As I catch up to her and try to touch her my hand goes completely through her. She has no solid presence, just elusiveness ... I sense how I felt towards my own mother ... The woman in the forest is my mother ... I feel so empty and sad ..."

As a child, this individual longed for his mother's affection. However, she paid more attention to her pet cats than she did him, and, to this day, his spirit remains starved for the bright spark of motherly nurturing.

~ ~ ~

"... I feel my entire body encased by this jelly-like mass ... I sense it pulsing, breathing ... It has a life of its own ... I'm trapped and weighted down by its heaviness ... Inside the mass I see and feel these small black insects feasting on my skin ... I can feel them furiously squirming, competing with each other for the privilege of tearing into my flesh. Help me , please! Yuck. I'm being eaten alive! Get them off! ..."

After this experience, this client explored its meaning with me. "Although I don't have all the clear memories, this visualization stunned me with its meaning. I know now that my body and soul still reek with the toxic touch of my sexually abusive father. It was the poisons from his hands that ate away at my childhood innocence and surrounded me with ugliness. Although my whole life I've kept such vileness hidden from sight, I know I must bring forth the truth, and cleanse the venom and vermin from my past, before they totally devour me."

7

Giving It Back to the Source: Methods of Feedback

After becoming intellectually aware of your source, and emotionally reliving the traumas, you are now ready to complete the purging process. Such completion requires that you give back your surfaced "stuff" to those who are responsible for its creation. You must effectively confront your source.

Such confrontation can be difficult and frightening, especially if you've spent years stuffing down your feelings. You may be well into adulthood before you feel ready to face a source from your childhood. I have found the feedback model described by Joe Wittmer and Robert Myrick in their book *"The Teacher as Facilitator"* (©1989, Educational Media Corporation) to be a helpful guide during this difficult final phase. This method instructs you to focus on how your source's specific behavior made or makes you feel. By giving examples of that specific behavior, expressing your feelings about it, and telling what your feelings make you want to do, you are explaining to your source the impact of his or her actions. To aid you in using this model, I have incorporated its three components into a simple feedback statement:

(Name of source), when you *(specific behavior of source)*, I feel *(your feeling)*, and I want to *(your resulting action)*.

The following examples show effective use of this model in action.

• *Mom*, when you *closed your bedroom door and shut me out*, I felt *rejected, angry, and isolated*, and *I wanted to shout at you*, "*Why don't you love me?*"

• *Mom and Dad*, when you *ignored me at the dinner table*, I felt *hurt and angry*, and it made me want to *invent a way to get your attention*.

• *Dad*, when you *violated me sexually*, I felt so *enraged and ashamed*, that I wanted to *get a gun and kill you*.

• *Mom*, when you *yelled at me for wetting the bed*, I felt so *humiliated*, that I wanted to *run away from home*. I was so *afraid* of your *tirades* that I actually *couldn't face any adult women*.

• *John*, when you *criticize the clothes I wear*, it makes me feel *angry*. I sense that you are *treating me like your child rather than your wife*. I feel *resentful* and I want to *be far away from you*.

• *Sarah*, when you *interrupt me*, I feel *frustrated*, and I want to *stop talking to you*.

• *Tom*, when you *walked out of my life without so much as a good-bye* I felt so *betrayed and abused*, that I wanted to *find some way to hurt you as much as you hurt me*. I felt *worthless and sickened* at the thought that I could mean so little to you.

Remember, this model is only a guideline in giving feedback. Keeping in mind the three components, you choose the words and order that would be most meaningful for your purging.

Giving feedback has often been extolled by other counseling theories as a virtuous method of enhancing communication between individuals. Although an enriched relationship may be a secondary outcome, the main purpose of feedback in SCT is to complete *your* cleansing process. If you have expectations of changing or enriching the individuals who are your source, you might be greatly disappointed. Remember, the purpose of feedback is to release and complete, not to change or control. Also, when giving feedback it is crucial that you do it with *feeling and intensity.* Just to say the words without the powerful feelings behind them will not totally complete the process. *Feeling* with feedback is your final regurgitation.

Although direct *face to face* feedback is the most powerfully effective, there are times when such personal contact is not possible. Death, distance, and refusal of your source to meet with you are some of the reasons which may require creative, more indirect alternatives.

For many people the telephone has proved to be a marvelous asset in bridging the mileage gap. Although not enabling you to have direct physical contact with your source, the telephone still provides the opportunity for you to verbally release your feelings. However, besides not providing a physical presence, it has another drawback. Since your source might react defensively and not be open to hearing you, he or she may choose to hang up the phone. This, in turn, may leave you frustrated in the present and prevent releasing your past. If you manage to catch them before they hang up or end the conversation, you have the healthy option of giving them feedback about their *current* behavior, so you don't stuff that down as well. For example: "Mom, when you act so hostile and hang up the phone when I try to tell you how I felt as a child, I feel dismissed, frustrated and unsafe to express myself. That makes me want to stay away from you."

If your source is still not willing to listen, or if the dialogue ends before you have the chance to give such current feedback, other alternatives of reaching your source and completing this process are still available. Writing a letter is one of them.

The following letter shows one approach to communicating with a source that has proved uncooperative. Here a woman writes her father. In past attempts to reach him, he may have walked away, hung up the phone, or laughed at her when she tried to speak with him.

Dear Dad:

Beginning this letter has been one of the most difficult feats I have ever attempted to accomplish. I realize that my feelings for you are so intense that I have been unwilling to experience the pain associated with expressing them. These feelings have been with me for years and color all my memories of us. The time has come for me to share them with you.

Dad, I only wish with all my heart that what I had to say would make you proud of me, something I've wanted my whole life. If only once you recognized me, or payed attention to my quiet withdrawal. I often wonder if you know the color of my hair or my eyes. I do not know if you've ever considered what's important to me. You instilled such terror in me and controlled me with that terror. As a result, my feelings were buried real deep many years ago. God, the pain has been excruciating.

I loathe you for what you did, you bastard. My insides still feel terror. I hardly survive the slightest imperfection about myself. Your unwillingness to accept me has created that same unwillingness in myself.

I still fear you and your rage to this day. I'm furious as to the pain you caused me and my mother.

At times, you tried to buy my respect with money and presents. I don't even know what you wanted at those times. What I do know is what I wanted from you. And it wouldn't have cost any money at all. Just someone to be my daddy. Oh God, to be held just once by a father's warm and caring arms. To feel protected, nurtured and loved. You could never do that for me. As a result, I feel orphaned. I feel I'm missing a part of life itself. I pray God continues to grace me with the gentle and tender men that surround me, accept me and care for me. I also pray that I can stop punishing them for your *cruel* behavior.

I want to be free of you, Dad. I want to be free of that sick repulsion, tightness, and gripping tension that twists the core of my being. I want to rid myself of the pain you've caused me, and will continue working to do so. I know my completeness with you will come. As difficult as this is for me, as painful as it feels, I trust I will someday be free; free to fully love, free to be loved, and free to fully experience my gift of life. Maybe not with a daddy, but with a pure and whole belief in myself that no one can ever take away again.

Your daughter

Parents are not necessarily the only individuals to cause us hurt. Friends, siblings, spouses, ex-spouses, lovers, ex-lovers, etc ... may be sources for us to complete with as well. This next letter is an example of how a letter might be written by someone who, for quite some time, has stored hurts caused by a former employer. Once the individual decides to release the resentment, and cleanse the wounds, a letter may be written directly to the source—here a previous boss.

Dear Bill:

I'm writing this letter to you in order to release some pain that still lingers in my heart. Confronting my sources of pain is a process I sincerely believe in. You are one of my sources, and I never gave you feedback directly. Perhaps I was too intimidated at the time. I no longer am intimidated and I no longer want to hold resentments that poison my soul.

Although currently successful and independent, I still have many mixed feelings about my years spent at the university. They are feelings that still haunt me.

Arriving at the university as a 30-year-old, I was filled with a fresh and youthful innocence. I was excited about teaching, and devoted to the concepts I was teaching. This combination of childlike innocence, excitement, and dedication was very effective when I taught. My enthusiasm seemed contagious, and the atmosphere in my classes seemed enchanted. Students felt safe to express what they thought and what they felt without fear of any consequences. They felt free enough to be creative and release their own childlike spirit that may have been dormant for so long.

I felt productive at the university and proud of my contributions. I was thrilled to be at a place where ideas flowed freely, learning was fun, and justice and idealism were paramount. Indeed, a university should be such a place. The world should look to a university as a producer of ideas and technology which constructively contribute to humanity. I felt lucky to be part of such an institution, with other great thinkers of our time.

Then, I began to have more contact with you. Although you claimed to be a supporter of mine, you were cold, intimidating, and critical of insignificant details. I felt a frigid bitterness from you. Only you know where that comes from. You overlooked my superb student evaluations and departmental reviews, and made only slight mention of my contributions as a teacher.

When I requested promotion and tenure long before the new president arrived, you refused, even though my department approved. Perhaps you felt that by threatening me with lack of tenure, I would produce more. According to all learning theories, production is increased by positive rewards, not by fear, intimidation, or threat. Again, however, only you know the reasons for your refusal.

My idealism was tarnished and I began to grow up. My innocence and childlike spirit were truly eroded. If a university was not a place for justice, truth, and integrity then I felt there were no places on earth for such virtues. I began to feel sad.

During my fifth year at the university, you finally did approve my tenure. However, it was too late. The new president had arrived. Your procrastination enabled a man I never met to go against the recommendations made by you, my department, and the student body. He denied me tenure, for whatever viciousness, anger, or bitterness lies in his soul. Again, only he knows. However, it is you who I blame for my departure from the university. If you were a true supporter of mine, you would have approved my attempts at receiving tenure long before this new president arrived.

As a result, I have no classes to dance with anymore. These dances should have been turned into full ballets. During my prime working years, which are now, I should have been making exciting national contributions with my combination of innocence, enthusiasm, and innovative ideas.

Although I mentioned that I have resentment towards you, most of my anger is gone. I feel sad and somewhat empty. I feel a loss. My innocence is gone. My enthusiasm towards life and my teaching seem also to be gone, or perhaps, just buried somewhere deep within me. I approach life with more caution, more weariness, and with none of the spontaneity others once found so endearing. I miss those parts of myself and miss touching others with them.

I write this letter not to condemn you, or to change you. If you choose, your changes can only come from you. I write this letter to release my sadness and resent-

ments. I want to purge my heart, cleanse my soul, free my
spirit, so I can once again dance with the world.

A former professor

In addition to, or as a substitute for writing letters,
many people have successfully made use of modern
audio-visual technology in their process of giving feedback. Such individuals have chosen to complete with
their sources through audio cassettes, and/ or video
tapes. Some have actually faxed their feedback.

Many people have effectively made use of the
technique of role-playing to help them either complete
with deceased sources or practice feedback they plan to
give a living but intimidating source. Clients have often
used me, their friends, spouses, or other willing ac-
quaintances as substitute sources in this dramatic proce-
dure. Like good actors, they are able to imagine, visualize, and feel that the person who stands before them is
an embodiment of their source. As a result, they are able
to release their feedback with appropriate and effective
intensity.

One woman creatively used a sequence of methods
to give her deceased father feedback and complete her
process. After writing a feedback letter to her father, she
proceeded to burn the letter and scatter its ashes. Hoping
that the 'scorched words would reach her father in hell'
she still felt that she had more rage to release. Asking me
to stuff my clothes with protective pillows, she proceeded to pound me with her fists (with my permission).
Crying, she imagined me as her father and verbally
poured out the effects of his abuse. However, she still
did not feel completely purged.

Smashing, whacking, kicking, slamming, and
throwing a piece of modeling clay around the room, she
imagined it to be her father and cursed it. Finally, she
went to his grave, carrying the knife he often used to

threaten her with when she was a child. At the cemetery, she plunged the blade over and over into his burial plot. She didn't want him to rest. She wanted him to listen to her. For the first time in her life she had his attention, and for the next two hours proceeded to tell him of the damage he had caused. Only then did she feel complete.

8

The Story of Lindsey:
A Case in
Source Completion Therapy

For a rare few seconds, Lindsey felt at peace. The water sprayed from above and saturated her hair in a blanket of warmth. As it cascaded down her face and onto her body, the purifying liquid enveloped her protectively. Now she felt clean and safe. Outside of the shower stall, Lindsey felt dirty and scared. With her eyes closed, Lindsey revelled in the moment. She loved her showers and took at least five a day.

The thunderous crash rocked Lindsey out of her reverie. Lindey's hands quickly covered her ears to shut out the roar and her startled eyes erupted in a stream of tears at a speed equal to the pouring shower head. Once warm from the shower, her body instantly began to shiver with a cold fear. Was she about to be the helpless victim of some sort of attack?

With tremendous effort, Lindsey forced herself to remove her hands from her ears and spread open the shower curtain. Trembling at what she might discover, she searched the bathroom but found nothing unusual. Then Lindsey glanced down at her feet and smiled. The bar of soap had slipped from its dish and fallen to the floor. That was her loud crash. Temporarily relieved, she turned off the water and exited from the shower.

Although calmer now, Lindsey knew that her intense fear was still very much alive somewhere inside her. As she towel-dried her body, she was aware that this paralyzing fright would, at times, continue to re-awaken. But, for now, she didn't want to think about it. Instead, Lindsey focused on her upcoming weekend at the casinos of Atlantic City. Outside of the shower, the casinos were her favorite place to be ...

Lindsey's body parts were busy. Her left hand alternately guided a cigarette and a vodka tonic toward her mouth. She inhaled the smoke and swallowed the alcohol, while her right hand placed the coins in the slot machine, then quickly pulled its handle. Stimulated, Lindsey's heart beat with excitement as her eyes stared at the combinations of fruit patterns that spun before them. Coin after coin, the fruits whirred in a sensuous dance, mesmerizing Lindsey with their seductive movements. Smoke after smoke and drink after drink, Lindsey's fear was buried deeper and deeper. Entranced, she remained at the machine from early morning till late at night, stopping for absolutely nothing, not even food. Her hypnotic addictions were her only nourishment.

So strong was Lindsey's desire to remain numb that her years of drinking, smoking, gambling and intense fear were not enough to motivate her to seek help. It took another murky encounter in the pure water of Lindsey's shower that led her into counseling.

In addition to cleansing her own skin, Lindsey was fastidious about scrubbing away the contaminants that clung to her own sons. Each evening, after her own purifying ritual, Lindsey would rub, wash, and scour each of her three boys from youngest to oldest. No crevice, pore, hair follicle, or fingernail would escape Lindsey's obsession to rid the family of pollutants.

The cleansing of her youngest son went fine, and his skin gleamed with a rosy hue as he left the bathroom. But the washing of her second son created the incident that changed Lindsey's life.

As his mother mechanically shampooed the hair on Shawn's head, he winced in discomfort ...

"Mommy, I have soap in my eyes! They're burning! Get me a towel ... Quick!"

Lindsey felt an immediate surge of power rush through her body, heating it with energy. She didn't like Shawn's demanding tone. In fact, she hated it. But, what happened next totally stunned her.

A rage emanating deep within her ballooned outward and filled the extremities of Lindsey's body. Her left hand closed tightly around Shawn's hair and her right hand held him by the throat. As she squeezed with a mighty force, Shawn gurgled in a panic, "Mommy, let me out ... I want to get out of here! You're hurting me!! Stop!!! ..." Lindsey didn't stop. Instead, she squeezed harder and held Shawn's head under the shower. Lindsey's fury was out of control. Her son gasped for breath, struggling to survive her choking hand and the drowning water.

Slipping and sliding, Shawn banged his head on the tiled shower wall and helplessly thumped to the floor. Observing her frightened and fallen son, Lindsey began to weep. Shocked back into control, she was able to subdue her rage. Almost automatically, she picked him up, dried him off, and apologized. However, Lindsey continued to weep for weeks. Intensely guilty, shocked, puzzled and frightened by her loss of control and its consequences, Lindsey decided to seek help and called me to begin her process.

Lindsey spent her first session with me describing the shower incident. As she related the story, Lindsey looked downward, cupped her head in her hands, and sobbed continuously. Every so often her muffled voice would plead her despair; "I don't want to hurt my babies ... I'm just so ashamed ... Please help me!! ..."

Periodically, her begging brown eyes would glance upward, imploring me to stop her pain. Lindsey's eyes were indeed "windows to her soul." Not only did they speak of her current guilt and desperation, they expressed past pain that still haunted her.

I asked Lindsey where her intense rage came from. She responded that she didn't know and that's what she wanted me to tell her. She wanted me to reassure her that she wasn't "crazy," and if she was, Lindsey wanted me to *cure* her. She wanted me to prevent her from ever acting that way with her son again. I, in turn, replied; "*Only you* know where your intense anger comes from. You're just not consciously aware yet." With that, we ended our first session.

For a number of months, Lindsey continued to focus on her outward symptoms and look to me for relief. However, I persisted in asking her to search beneath these symptoms and explore the purpose of them. Slowly, over the next year, she was able to gain more and more awareness of the past. Exploring Lindsey's intense transference towards me was one of the pathways to her past. During many sessions, she would keep her coat on, tightly clutching and wrapping it around her body. If I moved closer to her in any way, she would jerk away and shiver. Looking into her expressive eyes I sensed the presence of a frightened child.

At the completion of one session, we both rose from our chairs and I followed behind Lindsey, intending to open the door. I was startled as she turned around and spit forth the rage that abided within her. It was the same anger that blasted from her hands and held her son captive in the shower. Baring her teeth, Lindsey snarled; "Don't you ever come near me again ... I'll kick you.

You have no right to approach me. Stay away!! Stay away from me!! You have no f_____ right!! ..."

In subsequent sessions, I continued my efforts to help Lindsey examine the source of her rage and asked; "Where does it come from? Who are you really angry at? What does it do for you to be angry at me? Calmer, and not locked in transference, Lindsey began to get some of the answers.

"Although I can't remember all the details, I know my father was an alcoholic. He had his own business and wasn't around much. When he did come home, the whole house would scramble and panic. My mother would make sure everything was in its proper place, and I would run to my room and shut the door. I don't remember what happened to my brother, but I do remember being scared ... That's all I can recall right now. It's as if the rest of my childhood never existed. I do know, however, that I'm often both scared and furious at men with whom I have no significant relationship."

"How so?", I asked Lindsey, and she proceeded to examine more specifics of her transference.

"When men stare at me in a shopping mall, or while I'm driving, or for that matter whenever a man looks at me I first feel frightened. It's as if I expect to be attacked or hurt in some way. I feel so vulnerable and sense that I'll just be a powerless victim, frozen and even unable to scream for help. I'll be at his mercy. Then, I start to get angry.

"At times, I even feel my body enlarging, and expanding with a boiling rage. Usually, except in that instance with my son, I'm able to control it. I imagine lining up all the men in the world and cutting off their genitals with a sharp saber. Placing them in a blender, I watch the soupy mixture of blood and tissue spin rapidly until all traces of manliness disappear in the red liquid. With that fantasy, I get my power back. I feel less paralyzed, and I'm able to continue functioning.

It doesn't only happen with strangers. Even with my own husband, I react. Most of the time I'm glad when he's at work. I feel uncomfortable when he tries to get close to me. If he touches me, I feel my anger begin to rise. However, since he's my husband, I try hard not to show it. Instead, I make my body numb and tolerate his touch until he's done.

Sex is rare for us. My three boys were produced from my desire to have a little girl. I dreamed of dressing my daughter in pretty clothes, pampering and protecting her. I saw us laughing, giggling and having fun together. I always saw her smiling, something I never remember doing as a kid. So, I tolerated my husband's intimacy to gain my daughter. But, she never came. I feel God punished me."

" For what? Where does that feeling come from?" I asked Lindsey.

"I'm not totally sure. I sense it has to do with my father. But, I still can't recall the details of my youth. Although I do love my sons, I find it difficult to hug them as well. I know that I'm not as affectionate with them as they would like."

Lindsey, with my prodding, began to understand the purpose of her transference. "As long as I stay angry at other men I don't have to remember and feel the past pain caused by my father. I can focus completely on them and stay safe from my real hurts."

"Where does that keep you," I would ask.

"It keeps me stuck like a child, reacting to all men as if they were my father. With such anger and feelings of intimidation, I remain incapable of having the pleasure of a mature, adult relationship."

Although her conscious still resisted many painful past memories, Lindsey's desire for emotional health kept her committed to her therapeutic process. Such determination forced her conscious to be less and less resistant to the increasing number of messages sent by her subconscious. As soon as clues came into awareness, Lindsey explored their meaning. As understanding and awareness continued to unfold, reliving began to occur as well. In the next year or so of her process, she alternated between the awareness and reliving phases of SCT.

Lindsey's body language was one method used by her subconscious to communicate. During one particular session, exploration of Lindsey's physical language led to the alternation between awareness and reliving that I just mentioned. Lindsey began this session by tearing up one tissue into smaller pieces. She folded each piece into a tight, compact little package and placed them under her legs. I asked her, "What are your fingers saying?," and "What are you trying to hide?"

"I know a big part of me still wants to keep the pain and fear of my past tightly hidden away. I sense it coming up and I want to push it back down." She responded by rubbing both her wrists. When I asked her what her hands were saying, Lindsey began to relive a terrifying experience.

"It's just so dark in here. I'm so scared. Daddy made these ropes too tight and they hurt my wrists. I want to get out of here, but I'm too scared to scream. Daddy would get madder. Please!! ... Someone get me out! ... Take me out of this closet. I'm so cold... I won't be bad ever again... Mommy, Mommy, please..." Lindsey sobbed for the rest of the session.

The next time we met Lindsey's eyes immediately began to scour my office. Picking up tiny pieces of lint that littered my carpet, Lindsey disposed of them in my garbage can and then dusted my furniture with her hands. Before she sat down, Lindsey smoothed out each wrinkle on the cushion of the chair. When I asked her what her body was doing, Lindsey began to tell me about this compulsion.

"I know that at home I like everything to be perfect; everything must be in order, in its proper place. If a chair is moved, if a pillow is mussed, if an ashtray isn't where it's supposed to be I get angry at my family, and spend the time regaining order. I clean the bathrooms and vacuum the whole house once a day. I go crazy if my kids leave glasses or dishes in their rooms."

"Where does your need for perfection come from? What does it do for you?" I asked.

"First of all, I never wanted to get locked in that closet again. Daddy liked everything neat and tidy when he came home. I wanted to be good for him. I didn't want to be bad anymore and get punished. It was one of the only ways I could control my environment and stay safe from harm. You see, my brother and mother weren't as perfect and did not stay as safe. My brother never could seem to do anything right and was constantly getting beaten. When my father was drunk even my brother's laughter would provoke him and turn merriment into horror," she responded as another childhood memory surfaced with enough clarity and intensity for her to relive it.

"My mother crashed to the floor as he pushed her aside and bolted toward my brother. I see her strewn on the floor, lying so helpless. We're all so helpless. I watch his big hands move up and down and feel my body trembling. I can't see my brother, but I hear his curdling screams ... I can hear the smacks. Oh, so horrible! ... I see and hear the water from his bath splash against the sides of the tub. I know my brother is somehow trying to protect himself from this monster. I also know that he'll have big red hand prints over his body that will last for hours. I'm angry. I wish I could do something. I'm just too little and too scared. I don't want to be hit like that. I'll just be good and perfect."

Returning to the present, Lindsey continued by saying, "When I was younger my compulsion for order and perfection kept me safe from my father. As I grew it kept me removed from what I just reexperienced. The time and energy I spend cleaning helps me keep those buried memories and feelings out of my conscious. But, I continue to approach the world just as I did as a child; frightened and helpless. My father's behavior really affected my life in so many ways..."

Lindsey began to remember her dreams, particularly one recurring and terrifying nightmare. Upon retelling it in session, she allowed herself to feel its intensity and relive it in my office.

"I see this pretty little blond girl shaking in bed, keeping the blanket pulled up to her chin. She wants no parts of her exposed. She's so afraid that something terrible is about to happen. I can feel her fear. She's me. She looks like I did as a child.

I hear the creaking stairs and I know he's stepping up towards my bedroom. My heart is beating so fast I feel it will burst through my chest. Just for an instant, I see him at the doorway and cover my head with the blanket. I want to scream, but nothing comes out. I just want him to go away."

"What does he look like?" I asked.

"I just saw him for a second, but I know he's wearing a hat and a dark suit. I can't make out his face. It's hazy to me. I feel so alone; so vulnerable and unprotected. Where's my mother? ..."

At this point, I sensed Lindsey's need for silence to allow herself to stay with these vivid images and feelings. When she was ready, she ended the reliving experience and spoke about its aftermath.

"I always wake up drenched in sweat, my heart still thumping rapidly, and my body trembling uncontrollably. Although I see my husband sleeping next to me, I feel no sense of comfort. I still feel unsafe. You know, that's just like I felt at home. My mother, although alive and present, provided no protection from my tyrannical father. I feel angry at her too."

Eventually, the face in Lindsey's dream appeared clearly to her. It was the face of her father. "He continues to haunt me. The terror he instilled remains inside me to this very day. I want to get him out. I want to be rid of him and the agony he's caused me. I want to be free to enjoy what's left of my life."

Lindsey's dream also helped her clearly see the purpose of her many diversions. "For so long I wanted to stay removed from feeling the pain my father caused. Like the face in the dream, I wanted to stay hazy. I didn't want to see and feel the festering wounds from my past. My chain smoking literally kept me in a cloudy haze, while my drinking drowned out any feelings that might emerge. Gambling kept me in a mesmerizing stupor, while my showers were my attempts to wash away and cleanse the hurts. I know now that I must face, confront and deal with both my father and my feelings in order to purge them completely."

During her fourth year in therapy, Lindsey's attracting transference towards me aided her in discovering additional feelings. As her feelings of trust and safety with me increased, she began to ask me for tender hugs. "How come you want such affection from me?" I asked.

Lindsey explored that as well:

"I feel so sad. In addition to being scared and angry, I was also cheated. I was deprived of a father's gentle love, caring, compassion, and bonding intimacy. I remember now that wherever I went as a child I would intently notice all well-dressed and soft-spoken men. I dreamed that each one could be my father and fill my aching heart with love. So, I have the pain of my father's abuse as well as the emptiness of what he *didn't* provide."

Lindsey spent a good deal of her fourth year with me preparing to confront her parents. At first, she would pound the pillows in my office, cursing and screaming at them as if they were her parents. Releasing some of her boiling rage in this manner, she then began to role-play with me. As if I were her father, Lindsey spewed forth her feedback. She told of how "my" behavior made her feel so fearful, empty, angry, and helpless.

Next, Lindsey wrote letters to both her parents, which they were willing to read. Their receptiveness gave Lindsey the strength and encouragement to confront them face to face.

First, she met with her father and began the final phase of her process. Lindsey shared with me some of the statements she included in this feedback.

"Dad, when you drank, and came home late at night, I was terrified of you. I wanted to sink into my bed and just stay hidden. I wanted someone to stop you, but I felt too powerless."

"Dad, I just hated you when you hit Johnny. He was so innocent and small."

"Dad, when you locked me in the closet, the terror I felt in there remained with me until now. I often still feel the ropes around my wrists. I was so scared, that, as I grew, I drank, smoked and gambled just not to feel the horror. I remained frightened of all men most of my life. I want you to know how you affected me and I want to release these feelings back to you."

Next, Lindsey confronted her mother—

"Mom, when Daddy hurt us, I wondered where you were. I felt so alone and unprotected. I wanted you to rescue me, and I'm angry that you didn't."

During her fifth year in therapy, Lindsey continued to give her parents feedback about additional incidents she would recall. She persisted until she felt completely purged.

When Lindsey began the feedback phase she understood that this part of the SCT process was necessary for her to feel complete. We also discussed the possibility that her parents might not be open to such feedback. Knowing that she only needed to do this for herself, regardless of their reaction, Lindsey forged ahead with her feedback. To her surprise and delight, her parents displayed a willingness to listen and mend wounds from the past. Thus, Lindsey enjoyed a bonus. She was able to complete her purging process with her sources, as well as open the door to a closer relationship with them.

Currently, Lindsey no longer uses drinking, gambling and smoking as diversions. She is no longer frightened of men and enjoys an intimate sexual relationship with her husband. Lindsey has a professional service clean her house, and takes just one or two showers a day. Sudden noises no longer terrify her. Best of all, according to Lindsey, "I never lost control with my sons again, and I get pleasure from hugging them. I feel like I've been re-born and have another chance at life."

Parting Thoughts

As you voyage across the three phases of Source Completion Therapy, toward your destination of emotional health, please take note that the 3 phases do not always flow freely and clearly from one stage to the next. They often intertwine and overlap. For example, you may be in the process of reliving an event, which in itself, could ignite additional memories. These memories, in turn, need to be relived as well. The same concept applies to feedback. You may optimistically believe that you are at the point of finishing your process with feedback. However, giving feedback may also trigger more awareness and more memories to relive. Remember, this process takes time and commitment. There are no shortcuts to true emotional well-being.

Your diversionary behaviors will indicate your level of completeness with the process. They will diminish as you work through the phases, and vanish when you've finished.

SCT can also be used as a lifelong blueprint for emotional cleansing. If you attempt to block out current experiences and bury the painful feelings which accompany them, diversionary behaviors may, once again, spring up. If so, seek their source, relive the events, and complete the process by giving effective feedback.

Other Family Problem-Solving Books
... From Mills & Sanderson, Publishers

Recovering from Sexual Abuse and Incest: A Twelve-Step Guide, by Jean Gust and Patricia D. Sweeting. Two survivors collaborated to create this first-of-its-kind adaptation of the twelve steps of Alcoholics Anonymous to the unique needs of recovering victims of sexual abuse and incest. $9.95

Pulling Together: Crisis Prevention for Teens and Their Parents, by Dr. Harold D. Jester, with a foreword by Jacob Roseman, M.D. A veteran family counselor offers easy-to-follow advice to help teens and their parents learn to get along together and appreciate each other's good points. $9.95

The Big Squeeze: Balancing the Needs of Aging Parents, Dependent Children, and YOU, by Barbara A. Shapiro, Ph.D., with Vicki Konover and Ann Shapiro. An 8-step survival plan for dealing with the simultaneous needs of the three generations. $12.95

The Suddenly Single Mother's Survival Guide, by L. Patricia Kite. A modern-day guide to life after hubby, this delightful book is book informative and honest, offering advice on all that ails the single-again mother. $9.95

Childbirth Choices in Mother's Words, by Kim Selbert, M.F.C.C., with a foreword by noted childbirth author Carl Jones. These personal stories offer expectant parents a look at the various birthing options currently available in the United States. $9.95

Bedtime Teaching Tales for Kids: A Parent's Storybook, by Gary Ludvigson, Ph.D. You'll find no gentler way of helping young children (5-11) come to grips with serious problems than these 18 engrossing narratives intended to be read to the child at bedtime. $9.95

Winning Tactics for Women Over Forty: How to Take Charge of Your Life and Have Fun Doing It, by Anne DeSola Cardoza and Mavis B. Sutton. Written especially for those women jolted from the traditional marry-early, stay-at-home lifestyle by the women's movement, this book offers explicit advice on health, personal growth, financial planning, housing options, and more. $9.95

We gladly accept consumer orders by telephone.
Just call 800-441-6224.
We can bill you with shipment, or—if you prefer—charge
your purchase to your MasterCard or Visa.
OR ... you may send a note telling us which book(s) you
would like and enclosing full payment for the book, plus $1.50
per copy for shipping/handling.
Mail your order to: *Mills & Sanderson, Publishers*
*41 North Road, Suite 201 * Bedford, MA 01730-1021*